Cambridge Elements

Elements in Critical Heritage Studies
edited by
Kristian Kristiansen
University of Gothenburg
Michael Rowlands
UCL

WILL HERITAGE SAVE US?

Intangible Cultural Heritage and the Sustainable Development Turn

Chiara Bortolotto
Centre National de la Recherche Scientifique

Shaftesbury Road, Cambridge CB2 8EA, United Kingdom

One Liberty Plaza, 20th Floor, New York, NY 10006, USA

477 Williamstown Road, Port Melbourne, VIC 3207, Australia

314–321, 3rd Floor, Plot 3, Splendor Forum, Jasola District Centre,
New Delhi – 110025, India

103 Penang Road, #05–06/07, Visioncrest Commercial, Singapore 238467

Cambridge University Press is part of Cambridge University Press & Assessment,
a department of the University of Cambridge.

We share the University's mission to contribute to society through the pursuit of education, learning and research at the highest international levels of excellence.

www.cambridge.org
Information on this title: www.cambridge.org/9781009509091

DOI: 10.1017/9781009509114

When citing this work, please include a reference to the DOI 10.1017/9781009509114

First published 2025

A catalogue record for this publication is available from the British Library

ISBN 978-1-009-50909-1 Hardback
ISBN 978-1-009-50910-7 Paperback
ISSN 2632-7074 (online)
ISSN 2632-7066 (print)

Will Heritage Save Us?

Intangible Cultural Heritage and the Sustainable Development Turn

Elements in Critical Heritage Studies

DOI: 10.1017/9781009509114
First published online: February 2025

Chiara Bortolotto
Centre National de la Recherche Scientifique

Author for correspondence: Chiara Bortolotto, chiara.bortolotto@cnrs.fr

Abstract: Drawing on extensive ethnographic engagement with the social world of the UNESCO Convention for the Safeguarding of the Intangible Cultural Heritage, this Element explores the mainstreaming of sustainable development principles in the heritage field. It illustrates how, while deeply entwined in the UN standardizing framework, sustainability narratives are expanding the frontiers of heritage and unsettling conventional understandings of its social and political functions. Ethnographic description of UNESCO administrative practices and case studies explain how the sustainabilization of intangible cultural heritage entails a fundamental shift in perspective: heritage is no longer nostalgically regarded as a fragile relic in need of preservation but as a resource for the future with new purposes and the potential to address broader concerns and anxieties of our times, ranging from water shortages to mental health. This might ultimately mean that the safeguarding endeavor is no longer about us protecting heritage but about heritage protecting us.

This Element also has a video abstract:
www.cambridge.org/bortolotto_abstract

Keywords: UNESCO, intangible cultural heritage, sustainable development, global governance, standardization

ISBNs: 9781009509091 (HB), 9781009509107 (PB), 9781009509114 (OC)
ISSNs: 2632-7074 (online), 2632-7066 (print)

Contents

Introduction: Intangible Cultural Heritage, Endangerment, and Prospective Loss

"Minister (. . .) aren't you afraid for your children, your grandchildren?" This is how a young climate activist concluded her emotional intervention, sparking an equally passionate response on the part of the Italian Minister of the Environment in the summer of 2023, a time of unprecedented onslaught of extreme heat, floods, and wildfires across Europe. Bursting into tears, the activist stated suffering from "eco-anxiety"[1] and a fear of "not having a future." Along with eco-anxiety, new emergent forms of psychopathology include eco-shame, eco-phobia, eco-paralysis, eco-burnout, and eco-trauma, capturing the attention of psychiatrists and psychologists alike (Cianconi et al., 2023). These kinds of mental distress emerge within the contemporary struggle of navigating life in a "new climatic regime" (Latour, 2017) and resonate with an overarching "endangerment sensibility" (Vidal and Dias, 2016), where an anxiety about loss underpins human yearning for biological and cultural diversity (Berliner, 2018).

Against this backdrop, sustainability transformations embody "the dream of passing a livable earth to future generations, human and nonhuman" (Tsing, 2017: 51) and are regarded as the ultimate moral duty not only of political and institutional actors but of every individual. Increasingly fetishized in institutional and political discourse, the need to comply with sustainable development (hereafter SD) principles molds models of good governance relative to all aspects of everyday life – from waste management to food consumption and fashion design – to the point that the contemporary era has been described as the "age of sustainable development" (Sachs, 2015).

The imperative to preserve, rooted in the fear of extinction and so prominent in current SD narratives, has historically underpinned the heritage enterprise (Sodikoff, 2012). Archives, museums, and other conservation and documentary structures were designed to limit or avoid the loss of things past. From efforts to save the Nubian temples of Abu Simbel and Philae from rising waters of the Aswan dam (Betts, 2015) to campaigns for rescuing iconic landmarks like Venice or the Borobudur temple (to cite only the more grand international endeavors of the 1960s and 1970s), heritage thrived as a moral and political enterprise and as of part of a larger development narrative. Within this civilizing mission, in a modernist context shaped by the pursuit of progress and growth, heritage was about the preservation of things perceived as fragile and threatened (Meskell, 2018).

[1] The American Psychological Association refers to eco-anxiety as "a chronic fear of environmental doom" and explains that it entails clinical disorders like depression, rumination, anxiety, panic, substance abuse, and post-traumatic stress disorder (Clayton et al., 2017: 68).

However, in our current "catastrophic times" (Stengers, 2009) where the long-term survival of humankind has become a pressing concern (Tsing et al., 2017), heritage is no longer viewed solely as a fragile relic to be conserved. It is instead increasingly seen as a means for envisioning alternative modes of exploiting natural resources, strengthening social bonds, and sustaining the economy. In other words, we are witnessing a move from a scenario where heritage is the object of protection, regarded by the United Nations Educational, Scientific and Cultural Organization (UNESCO) as a duty of humanity, to a situation where humans themselves are seen as vulnerable and in need of protection and heritage a valuable resource in this regard. Observing the integration of sustainable development narratives and priorities in the heritage realms thus reflects a fundamental shift in perspective: it is no longer about us protecting heritage but about heritage protecting us. This Element explores this shift.

I investigate this crucial move within a specific domain of heritage – Intangible Cultural Heritage (hereafter ICH). ICH provides an exceptional window onto patterns of loss and the inverted temporality of the anxiety they spur, as we grapple with the specter of our own extinction. Notably, ICH broadened the conventional conceptualization of heritage, previously solely comprising monuments or sites to be faithfully conserved, to include cultural and social practices encompassing rituals, games, craftsmanship, or foodways, which are "constantly recreated." As defined in the UNESCO Convention for the Safeguarding of the Intangible Cultural Heritage (ICH Convention),[2] ICH encompasses "practices, representations, expressions, knowledge and skills [. . .] that communities, groups and, in some cases, individuals recognize as part of their cultural heritage" (UNESCO, 2003, art. 2.1). In emphasizing its living character, UNESCO's definition portrays ICH as a dynamic set of elements that "communities and groups" can reinvent "in response to their environment, their interaction with nature and their history" and that provide them "with a sense of identity and continuity" (ibid.).[3]

Besides normative texts, ICH is also shaped by prescriptive practices that define and delineate its boundaries, notably through inscriptions on the international lists established by the Convention – the Representative List and the List of ICH in Need of Urgent Safeguarding, known as the Urgent Safeguarding

[2] Accepted by the UNESCO General Conference in 2003. As of June 2024, it has been ratified by 183 states, referred to as "States Parties."

[3] The full definition furthermore highlights that, for the purposes of the Convention, ICH "is compatible with existing international human rights instruments, as well as with the requirements of mutual respect among communities, groups and individuals, and of sustainable development" (Art. 2.1).

List – as well as inclusion in national-level inventories.[4] These mechanisms play a pivotal role in shaping official representations of ICH. The international lists include a diverse array of items, more than 700, ranging from Turkish whistled language to Indonesian batik, Albanian folk iso-polyphony, Congolese rumba, Syrian shadow play, Colombian and Venezuelan Illano work songs, Mongolian coaxing rituals for camels, or the Brazilian capoeira circle. Inscriptions have increasingly seen the addition of elements explicitly associated with land or water management, healthcare, and social inclusion, thereby establishing, in practice, an explicit connection with sustainable development priorities.[5]

The concept of ICH departs from that of "Outstanding Universal Value," the key paradigm of the World Heritage framework. ICH relies, in fact, on a relativistic and particularistic interpretation of heritage, where specific groups are urged to exert their "heritage self-determination" (Bortolotto, 2015) and recognize the heritage value of what they perceive as a source of identity and continuity (UNESCO, 2003, art. 2; Bortolotto, 2011). Since its entry into force, the ICH Convention has become a model capable of influencing heritage policies more broadly, including World Heritage itself (Brumann, 2013). Due to its intrinsic relationship with the economy, the environment, and society, ICH is not only conceptualized as "living heritage" but also envisioned as an agent for change, introducing new issues and concerns into heritage policies that extend beyond conservation (Bortolotto, 2017b, 2021).

While heritage conservation sought to preserve traces of a vanishing past, the transmission of ICH is purportedly based on change and adaptation of contemporary practices to future priorities. ICH operates within a different temporality, where loss does not concern things of the past. To paraphrase the title of Meskell's book, what are to be protected for the future are not the ruins of

[4] Two lists are established by the Convention: The Representative List of the Intangible Cultural Heritage of Humanity and the List of Intangible Cultural Heritage in Need of Urgent Safeguarding. The former seeks to showcase the diversity of Intangible Cultural Heritage and enhance awareness of its significance. The latter aims to foster international collaboration and support for the safeguarding of cultural expressions deemed to require urgent measures to ensure their viability. Additionally, a Register of Good Safeguarding Practices includes programs, projects, and activities regarded as examples of effective safeguarding efforts. At the national level, States Parties are expected to draw up one or more inventories of the intangible cultural heritage present in their territories.

[5] The Intergovernmental Committee for the Safeguarding of Intangible Cultural Heritage makes decisions regarding inscription. Their assessments rely on the recommendations of an Evaluation Body, appointed by the Committee, consisting of six experts from States Parties not part of the Committee and six representatives from accredited non-governmental organizations. These individuals, including diplomats or experts, are periodically involved with the ICH Convention, even if their primary everyday responsibilities are not always directly tied to the Convention or the field of ICH.

bygone civilizations (2018). These peoples have long disappeared, the loss has already happened, and thus here heritage protection is intended as a conservation of their remains. Losing ICH instead means losing the very possibility of its reenactment and therefore of the continuous existence of particular aspects of contemporary, yet often marginalized, civilizations. In other words, the loss not only is behind us but also lies ahead. It is yet to come (Tornatore, 2017).

These concerns, particularly the need to anticipate loss (DeSilvey and Harrison, 2019), resonate with ecological apprehension amid a growing awareness of and distress over the fragility of human livelihoods on our crowded, unequal, and devastated planet. Rather than particular cultural practices, what is perceived as fundamentally endangered is the very possibility of human life on earth. Similar to the protection of biodiversity, the safeguarding of ICH is seen as a future-oriented responsibility: a way to proactively envision new possible destinies in terms of livelihoods, the relationship with nature, and interaction with the environment. The promotion of knowledge and skills transmission from previous generations in this context is not driven by a melancholic longing for a bygone world. Like the "eco-nostalgia" underpinning the safeguarding of biological material in order to keep it available for future generations who will face famine and displacement (Angé and Berliner, 2020), the safeguarding of ICH is not meant to be past-oriented. Embodying a form of "anticipatory heritage" (Kirshenblatt-Gimblett, 2024), it intends to encourage innovative action and manifest a "yet unrealized future potential" to cope with crises (Bargheer, 2016: 116). In essence, ICH is endorsed as a conceivable catalyst for expanding our imaginations and a window onto how social and institutional actors might envision and negotiate sustainability solutions.

In exploring the intersection between ICH and SD, my intention is not to reiterate UNESCO's normative discourse or propose practical approaches for advancing the SD agenda. Instead, I delve into what SD does to heritage and vice versa. Specifically, I examine how thinking of ICH in SD terms changes our understanding of heritage and of its social and political function, and conversely, how ICH is utilized by social and institutional actors as a resource for SD, influencing this field of action and its representations.

I argue that describing "how things are" rather than "how they ought to be" (Monsutti, and Pétric, 2009: 13) facilitates a better understanding of these shifts. This in turn allows the formulation of practical answers useful in activist struggles for sustainability. In this sense, an analytical stance has a critical function and an engaged ambition, as it sheds light on the "various ways in which heritage now has a stake in, and can act as a positive enabler for, the complex, multi-vector challenges that face us today, such as cultural and environmental sustainability, economic inequalities, conflict resolution, social cohesion and the future of cities, to name a few" (Winter, 2013: 533). In other words, in this Element I adopt a non-moralizing engagement with SD and heritage, tackling them as objects for inquiry rather than as concepts, without taking on as my own the representations of the actors who believe in sustainable development or heritage (Olivier de Sardan, 1995: 22). This form of "heritage agnosticism" (Brumann, 2014) or "analytical distanciation" (Larsen et al., 2022: 8) from normative perspectives comes with a twofold challenge: on the one hand, an epistemological responsibility to integrate scientific literature produced by practitioners and experts as an expression of emic views (Bierschenk, 2014: 90) and, on the other, an ethical duty to "engage up" (Ceribašić, 2019) with my interlocutors in order to critically support their struggles and elucidate conundrums over "how to do good" (Fisher, 1997; Jacobs, 2024: 59). In this view I combine an anthropological approach – able to assess the narratives entangling ICH and SD and better understand their agency in shaping social representations of the heritage enterprise – with a concern for understanding how heritage becomes a resource for imagining sustainable solutions for our future.

This Element also responds to a call for the anthropology of sustainability "to engage more systematically with international institutions and the policy-making bodies they spawn, [...] describe bureaucratic contexts, decode the discourses of different interest groups, map ambiguities and contradictions, and assess claims" (Brightman and Lewis, 2017: 22). Tracing the circulation of models within this network reveals how UNESCO's heritage programs "order" them to produce particular understandings of cultural transmission. This ordering is achieved through the interrelation of different agents: discursive, institutional, spatial, legal, regulatory, administrative, scientific, and moral, what Michel Foucault calls a *dispositif* (Foucault, 1975). I thus view UNESCO, the global and most influential incarnation of what Laurajane Smith (2006) calls the "authorized heritage discourse," not solely as an arena where heritage appears as an object of change and theoretical development but also as a powerful agent and an infrastructure enabling change.

My effort to comprehend the values shaping the norms underpinning heritage protection and the constant evolution of the heritage field builds on a long-term ethnographic engagement with the complex social world of the ICH Convention. Over the past twenty years, I have regularly conducted ethnographic observation of the governing bodies of the Convention, the General Assembly of the States Parties to the Convention and the Intergovernmental

Committee for the Safeguarding if the ICH, as well as participated in numerous "expert meetings" globally.[6] I have also been an actor in the very apparatus that I observe.[7] If spurring unsolvable "collaborative dilemmas" (Bortolotto, 2017a), this multi-positionality (Sapignoli, 2017: 80) within the ICH social world has allowed me to penetrate its affective life (Graham, 2002; Stoler, 2007; Laszczkowski and Reeves, 2015; Mathur, 2017; Billaud and Cowan, 2020; Bortolotto, 2024). Understanding UNESCO's action as an imperfect human endeavor makes it possible not only to better grasp its utopian momentum but also to nuance official representations of an international policy apparatus that presents itself as rational, emotionally neutral, consistent, and harmonious (Navaro-Yashin, 2006; Müller, 2013).

1 Intangible Cultural Heritage as an Object *of* Change

If what is regarded as "sustainable" is relative and culturally determined, the pursuit of "sustainability" is officially recognized as a shared concern for humanity. Over the last several decades, the international community has shaped the normative understanding of SD, establishing a set of principles that the world is expected to adhere to and purposes it is expected to aspire to. Throughout this process, the concept of SD has undergone successive reconceptualizations, where emphasis has shifted from a concern for intergenerational transmission to holistic ambitions integrating economic, social, and environmental aspects (Sachs, 2015). The commonly cited definition of SD by UN agencies and other international organizations originates from the Brundtland Report, named after the chairperson of the World Commission on Environment and Development, Gro Harlem Brundtland, where it is described as "development that meets the needs of the present without compromising the ability of future generations to meet their needs" (World Commission on Environment and Development, 1987). This emphasis on intergenerational transmission later influenced the principles of the Rio Declaration produced by the Rio Earth Summit in 1992 (United Nations, 1992). Twenty years later, the report generated from the Rio+20 Summit,

[6] For more than a decade, I have regularly attended the annual meetings of the Committee (Abu Dhabi, Bali, Paris, Baku, Windhoek, Addis Ababa, Jeju Island, Port Louis, Bogota, Rabat, Kasane, Asunción as well as Nairobi and Kingston/Paris on live webcast). I have also participated in the biannual sessions of the General Assembly of the States Parties at the UNESCO headquarters in Paris.

[7] Beyond observing the governing bodies of the Convention, I have actively participated in its implementation. Specifically, I have contributed to the development of the French inventory of ICH and, since 2012, have sat on the Ethnological and Intangible Heritage Committee, established to advise the French Minister of Culture on the implementation of the Convention. I have furthermore participated in a number of bids for inclusion on the UNESCO ICH lists in Italy and France, and served as a "facilitator" in several European countries within UNESCO's global capacity building program.

Realizing the Future We Want for All, would integrate an holistic ambition embracing economic, social, and environmental objectives, known as the "three pillars" of SD, as well as concerns for peace and security (UN system task team on the post-2015 UN development agenda, 2012). This same holistic ambition shapes the 17 Sustainable Development Goals (hereafter SDGs) of the 2030 Agenda for Sustainable Development adopted by the UN General Assembly in 2015 (United Nations, 2015).

As a UN agency, UNESCO has long sought to influence this Agenda. Labadi (2022) retraces UNESCO's call for a cultural turn in development since the 1970s, observing how the culture-for-development narrative originated in the Global South. The UNESCO narrative points out that the need to promote a culturally sensitive approach to development was highlighted as early as the 1982 MONDIACULT Conference, organized by UNESCO in Mexico (Arizpe, 2004). The official account of the Organization further highlights how this ambition was operationalized during the World Decade for Cultural Development (1988–1997) launched by UNESCO "to promote awareness of the cultural imperative" (Mayor, 1988: 6) and reflected in the report *Our Creative Diversity*, prepared by the World Commission on Culture and Development (1996) to offer a cultural counterpart to the Brundtland Report, *Our Common Future*, which focused instead on environmental concerns.

The constructive integration of culture, heritage, and development reflects UNESCO's desire to disseminate its policy agenda and strengthen its position within the UN system, in particular ensuring a prominent position for the World Heritage, ICH, and Cultural Diversity Conventions[8] within the UN normative framework (Vlassis, 2015). The role of cultural and creative industries, in particular, was valorized in terms of poverty reduction and employment, aligning notably with the pragmatic view of states in the Global South willing to consider heritage as an asset for generating resources, especially from cultural tourism (Wiktor-Mach, 2020: 320). The organization of the International Congress "Culture: Key to Sustainable Development," convened by UNESCO in Hanghzhou in 2013, is presented as a crucial step in this process. Financially supported by China, the conference emphasized the role of non-Western countries in the design of the culture-for-development UNESCO agenda (Wiktor-Mach, 2019, 2020). The resulting *Hanghzou Declaration: Placing Culture at the Heart of Sustainable Development Policies*, recommended "that a specific Goal focused on culture be included as part of the

[8] Convention concerning the Protection of the World Cultural and Natural Heritage (UNESCO, 1972), Convention for the Safeguarding of the Intangible Cultural Heritage (UNESCO, 2003), and Convention on the Protection and Promotion of the Diversity of Cultural Expressions (UNESCO, 2005).

post-2015 UN development agenda, to be based on heritage, diversity, creativity and the transmission of knowledge and including clear targets and indicators that relate culture to all dimensions of sustainable development."[9] This program, promoted by Irina Bokova during her tenure as UNESCO director-general (2009–2017), culminated in the Resolution on Culture and Sustainable Development adopted by the UN General Assembly in December 2013,[10] which requested that culture be given due consideration in the post-2015 development agenda.

These efforts were, however, only partially successful since no explicit goal dedicated to culture was ultimately included. Acknowledgment of the role of heritage for SD is limited to a specific "heritage target" (no. 11.4), which aims to "strengthen efforts to protect and safeguard the world's cultural and natural heritage." This target falls under the urban goal (no. 11) focusing on inclusive, safe, resilient, and sustainable cities and human settlements. Despite this, UNESCO has continued to advocate for a more robust role of culture to be incorporated into the post-2030 Agenda. This is the perspective that guided the meeting of Ministers of Culture from UNESCO Member States at the UNESCO World Conference on Cultural Policies and Sustainable Development – MONDIACULT 2022. Taking place forty years after the 1982 MONDIACULT Conference, the event reiterated a fundamental call for integrating culture and development. The final Declaration from the conference accordingly advocated for a "systemic anchoring of culture in public policies, through the adaptation of development strategies and frameworks" and urged the UN secretary General "to integrate it as a specific goal in its own right in the development agenda beyond 2030."[11]

UNESCO is not only an agent in attempts to shape the UN agenda, it is also shaped by it. The emphasis placed on the interrelation between culture and development has strategic significance, as it facilitates collaboration with other UN agencies while being a precondition for the Organization to access UN funding tied to development projects (Vlassis, 2015; Wiktor-Mach, 2020; Labadi, 2022). This became a particularly crucial aspect after the United States withdrew from the Organization in 2011, leading to suspension of the

[9] The Hangzhou Declaration: Placing Culture at the Heart of Sustainable Development Policies, Adopted in Hangzhou, People's Republic of China, on May 17, 2013.

[10] A/RES/68/223. [online] https://documents-dds-ny.un.org/doc/UNDOC/GEN/N13/452/83/PDF/N1345283.pdf?OpenElement (accessed November 11, 2023).

[11] MONDIACULT-2022/CPD/6. www.unesco.org/sites/default/files/medias/fichiers/2022/09/6.MONDIACULT_EN_DRAFT%20FINAL%20DECLARATION_FINAL_1.pdf?TSPD_101_R0=080713870fab2000b96c4b03779fbdec5af2782aee1b2a96c545f9a53abcf2ebc047fb83c0fd46ec08353f8a6c1430003fd964c1465dced6c5e9c55814baacba2553e05de3ca25d82c94f4c5ae474cf479ee4ff540eb6ef4eea8cb634940aeb8, p. 4; p. 7 (accessed November 11, 2023).

country's contributions. A retired UNESCO official, former chief of the ICH section, highlighted this pragmatic engagement with SD, pointing out that "if there's no sustainable development, we won't be able to work in the United Nations family: we'll have no funding, nothing. We have to go along with it, even if people don't agree." In this sense, UNESCO is indubitably an interesting arena for observing the mainstreaming of the 2030 Agenda and its SD narratives, along with their impact on representations of heritage.

1.1 The Rise of Sustainable Development within the Intangible Cultural Heritage Convention

Alignment with the SDGs has become an official priority for the Organization since the start of a reflection on the post 2015-SD program within the UN political arena (Bortolotto and Skounti, 2024). Heritage emerges here as an object *of* change, capable of reinterpreting itself and adapting to new priorities and values. Its agency is renewed in the light of SD, consolidating and incorporating inputs established as international policy goals within the UN. Observing these developments from within UNESCO allows us to grasp the organization's role as a clearinghouse for heritage policies, promoting their reinterpretation and subsequent global dissemination.

The *Convention Concerning the Protection of the World Cultural and Natural Heritage*, which emerged in the early 1970s when sustainable development was not yet a global buzzword, initially lacked references to SD. It was only thirty years later, with the adoption of the Budapest Declaration on World Heritage in 2002, that the concept of sustainable development was introduced. This declaration emphasized the need to integrate conservation into social and economic development (UNESCO, 2002). The growing importance of these concerns was further reflected in the theme chosen for the fortieth Anniversary of the World Heritage Convention in 2012: "World Heritage and Sustainable Development: the Role of Local Communities." To address the perceived partial engagement with SD within the context of the increasing centrality of the latter for the UN system (Labadi and Gould, 2015), a new *Policy on the Integration of a Sustainable Development Perspective into Processes of the World Heritage Convention* was adopted in 2015. The aim was to align all World Heritage procedures with the post-2015 UN Sustainable Development agenda (Boccardi and Scott, 2018).

The Convention for the Safeguarding of the Intangible Cultural Heritage instead came to life in a different historical moment, and does explicitly refer to

SD.[12] The preamble, which outlines the broad political lines of the treaty and provides exhortatory elements toward possible legal developments (Blake, 2020: 20), characterizes ICH as a "guarantee of sustainable development." Article 2.1 refers to SD in a *caveat* sentence that circumscribes the definition of ICH:

> For the purposes of this Convention, consideration will be given solely to such intangible cultural heritage as is compatible with existing international human rights instruments, as well as with the requirements of mutual respect among communities, groups and individuals, and of sustainable development.

That said, even though SD was mentioned in the text of the ICH Convention and the idea of sustainability was present in preparatory debates over the definition of ICH (Appréderisse, 2019), it wasn't a central concern for the drafters of the Convention (Smeets, 2024). SD thus remained largely "undefined" and only "nominally" a core pillar of the Convention for an extended period of time (Kono, 2007; Lixinski, 2014). As one of the main experts involved in the drafting of the Convention bluntly put it, its inclusion in the final formulation seemed like "a box-ticking exercise to acknowledge its place in international policy-making" (Blake, 2024: 21).

Indeed, while the official narrative claims that ICH is "at the heart of the Convention" (Curtis, 2017), ethnographic observations of the debates of the governing bodies of the Convention reveal that SD has not been a major or recurrent concern for many years. Interestingly, the first Secretary of the Convention noted that during his mandate (ended in mid-2008) he was neither asked by the UNESCO director-general to tackle SD in his work nor was "ICH and sustainable development a hot item for the Governing Bodies." This is confirmed by the very rare occurrences of the term SD "in many hundreds of pages of records of the first nine meetings of the Committee and General Assembly (2006–2010)."[13]

The evaluation conducted by the Internal Oversight Service of UNESCO in 2013 underlined that while the Convention's preamble asserted that ICH is a guarantee of sustainable development, there was no concrete evidence supporting this claim in either the Convention or the Operational Directives. It pointed out the "challenge" of "consciously building" linkages between ICH and sustainable development "in practice" or even "creating such linkages where they do not yet exist" (UNESCO, 2013: 15).

[12] Similarly, the Convention on the Protection and Promotion of the Diversity of Cultural Expressions (UNESCO 2005) makes of SD one of its guiding principles (Art. 2.6).

[13] Rieks Smeets, personal communication.

The first, if vague, references to the concept of SD were added to the Operational Directives (hereafter "ODs")[14] of the ICH Convention in 2010, and consisted of simply encouraging the media to contribute to "raising awareness about the importance of the intangible cultural heritage as a means to foster social cohesion, sustainable development and prevention of conflict, in preference to focusing only on its aesthetic or entertainment aspects" (OD 111). Initial debates within the governing bodies of the Convention, however, primarily discussed SD with a focus on the economic uses of ICH and related opportunities and risks.[15] This led to the adoption of a first set of new ODs addressing the potential of commercial activities involving ICH to "improve the living standards of the communities that bear and practice the heritage, enhance the local economy, and contribute to social cohesion" (OD 116). These new ODs furthermore highlighted the vital importance of sustainable tourism management where ICH is concerned (OD 117) and warned against "over-commercialization" and "unsustainable tourism" (OD 102).

It was only when a more comprehensive reflection was initiated on the interrelation between ICH and SD that other aspects of SD came to the fore. The discussion now not only focused on how ICH could serve as a source of livelihood but also addressed its potential contributions to the preservation of ecosystems and genetic biodiversity, provision of adequate nutrition, strengthening of health and well-being, optimization and management of water use, promotion of harmonious social relationships through social and festive events, and resolution of conflicts. In essence, a shift occurred when SD became a key priority on the United Nations agenda, prompting UNESCO to align its actions accordingly. UNESCO itself identified the somewhat marginal position of SD in the Convention as a "gap" and progressively emphasized the need to "research the relation between ICH and sustainable development (and vice versa) in more depth" (UNESCO, 2013: 15).

It was precisely to fill this gap that substantial additions were made to the ODs in 2016, which saw the introduction of a new chapter dedicated specifically to the linkages between intangible cultural heritage and sustainable development. The chapter frames the articulation between these two areas and seeks to guide States Parties to the Convention in promoting SD through ICH. Its structure, just like the policy document adopted by the AG of the World Heritage Convention, mirrors that of the 2030 Agenda, organized around three dimensions (social, economic and environmental) with the addition of

[14] The different versions of the OD are available on the website of the ICH Convention: https://ich.unesco.org/en/directives (accessed November 11, 2023).

[15] See, for example, the Decision of the Intergovernmental Committee ITH/13/8.COM/13.a. [online] https://ich.unesco.org/en/decisions/8.COM/13.A (accessed November 11, 2023).

a fourth dimension concerning peace and security. These dimensions encompass sub-issues such as education, health, food security, income generation, tourism, natural resource management, access to clean water, climate change, social cohesion, prevention and resolution of conflicts, and the reconstruction of collectives following conflicts.

The evolution of the ODs, which States Parties to the Convention can relatively easily develop to address new social and political priorities and needs, shows how this international standard has changed over time. In addition to these legal texts, the official narrative accompanying their regular updates also provides insight into the growing emphasis on SD within the ICH Convention. Specifically, the development of the Convention has been accompanied by official statements, articulated, for example, in the forewords to the so-called "blue book" containing the "Basic Texts" of the Convention, which is re-edited every two years when the ODs are updated. These paratextual narratives reflect the emergence of SD as a key concern within the UNESCO arena.

In the first edition of these texts, in 2008, Koïchiro Matsuura, who strongly championed the international institutionalization of ICH and enabled the rapid negotiations of the ICH Convention, made no reference to sustainable development. For Matsuura, ICH was first and foremost about introducing a counterpart to World Heritage while exporting at the global level the Asian, particularly Japanese, heritage values and system (Bortolotto, 2013). In 2010, Irina Bokova, who succeeded Matsuura and was actively involved in positioning UNESCO as a credible and crucial actor within the UN debate on the post-2015 agenda (Labadi, 2022),[16] placed great emphasis on SD. Her statement in the foreword serves as a political message, highlighting the importance of SD even more explicitly than the actual text of the OD the foreword introduces:

> Promoting the central role of culture, and more specifically living heritage, in sustainable development processes, is an issue that I ardently advocate, especially in the framework of the UN Millennium Development Goals. (…) Traditional knowledge systems and age-old wisdom can teach us many valuable lessons in such specific fields as food security, health and natural resource management and, more broadly, can contribute to maintaining social cohesion and peaceful co-existence. In addition, formal education should build on intangible cultural heritage to make school education more relevant to students while reinforcing identity and greater understanding and respect of cultural diversity. As regards sustainable economic development, traditional craftsmanship can generate income for families while providing their communities with activities in line with their own values and cultural contexts.

[16] From 2014 to 2016, Irina Bokova was a candidate for the position of UN Secretary-General.

Two years later, no further modifications with regard to SD were introduced within the ODs, but the foreword of the director-general nonetheless remains fully focused on the concept of SD and further highlights its centrality. With explicit references to this concept in the first and last sentences, this foreword can be seen as an explicit plea for making room for culture in the 2030 Agenda, which at the time was under discussion at the UN level:

> At a time when the world is seeking new ways to further peace and sustainable development, we have a need for unifying projects which bring us together in our diversity (...) Culture is a renewable resource par excellence and is thus a major dimension of sustainable development. Culture is a force for social inclusion and collective mobilization. Experience proves that the acknowledgement of cultural heritage in the design and conduct of development policies is a factor conducive to the active participation of communities and boosts the effectiveness of programmes in the longer term. As the United Nations works on the formulation of a new post-2015 development agenda it is time to recognize the transformative power of cultural heritage (...). The intangible cultural heritage provides direct access to the memory of peoples: it is a living source where responses can be found to the challenges of peace and sustainable development (...). I should like to take this opportunity to reaffirm UNESCO's determination to carry on with this work, in the firm belief that the intangible cultural heritage has a central role in the construction of peace and sustainable development.

While the 2014 edition did not introduce any relevant changes in either the ODs or its preface, the foreword to the 2016 edition announces that "several important elements of the Operational Directives were amended, such as an additional chapter on the linkages between intangible cultural heritage and sustainable development." In 2018, under the signature of Audrey Azoulay, the new director-general, the text further elaborates on the role of SD to "promote more sustainable ways of living together in resilient, inclusive and peaceful societies" and announces the launch of an "overall results framework for the Convention," a tool allowing "to measure and monitor the impact of the Convention at various levels, in the spirit of the 2030 Agenda for Sustainable Development."

The 2020 foreword to the Basic Texts also addresses sustainability issues, underlining the role of ICH for sustaining the "livelihoods and resilience" of communities. It emphasizes the importance of ICH as "a driver of strength, solidarity and hope" during the COVID-19 crisis and introduces a major development in the ODs concerning the role of ICH in emergencies, seen as "a powerful tool for resilience and recovery." Finally, in 2022, Audrey Azoulay insists on the role of ICH for SD: "More than ever, intangible heritage remains highly relevant – not only to promote peace and cultural diversity, but also to address challenges such as climate disruption. Every day, this heritage proves that *it is not fragile*, but truly alive" (emphasis added).

Signed by successive UNESCO DGs, these texts reflect distinct political agendas but also consistently illustrate how, since 2010, the representation of ICH and of its social role has shifted from "fragile" cultural expressions to be protected (see also Smeets, 2024) to a "resource" for SD. The "Seoul vision," a document elaborated following an expert meeting organized on the occasion of the twentieth anniversary of the Convention, explicitly endorses this agenda. This text advocates for future action to "fully realize the potential of intangible cultural heritage as an enabler of inclusive social and economic development and environmental sustainability, while also recognizing their interdependence with peace and human security." It promotes transversality in policy-making, highlighting the role of ICH in sustaining livelihoods, protecting biodiversity, and contributing to defining strategies for disaster risk reduction and climate change adaptation.[17]

1.2 Listing as a Prescriptive Practice

Beyond legal documents and official UNESCO discourse, the prescriptive representation of ICH and its field of application are shaped by heritage-making practices, where local and national heritage actors are more directly involved. Heritage lists and inventories play a performative role in this context, as the selection process underlying the listing gives particular cultural practices a heritage status whose legitimacy is sanctioned by local, national, or international heritage authorities, generating sometimes all sorts of instrumentalizations (Noyes, 2006; Hafstein, 2009; Foster, 2011; Chong, 2012; Aykan, 2016). These lists, along with the debates and controversies that accompany the inscriptions, clearly illustrate the ways in which the field of ICH has evolved over time. This is, for instance, evident in the case of food practices, which were initially absent from these lists and now make up a significant portion of them (Bortolotto, 2017b; Bortolotto and Ubertazzi, 2018).

The first elements inscribed on the UNESCO ICH lists in 2008[18] primarily consisted of dances, songs and other musical forms, theatre, storytelling, and carnivals, with few exceptions. Five years later, the lists – which included practices such as the Polyphonic singing of the Aka Pygmies of Central

[17] The Seoul Vision for the Future of Safeguarding Living Heritage for Sustainable Development and Peace. [online] https://ich.unesco.org/doc/src/61291-EN.pdf (accessed November 11, 2023).

[18] In 2008, items that had been proclaimed "masterpieces of the oral and intangible heritage of Humanity" in 2001, 2003, and 2005 within the framework of a previous UNESCO program were included in the Representative List.

Africa, the Royal ballet of Cambodia, the Sicilian Puppet Theatre, and the Samba de roda of the Recôncavo of Bahia – still resembled, in the words of a representative of a North American NGO, a "folkloric menu for tourists." During our flight from London to Baku, on our way to the Committee meeting, he commented that the priority should be for ICH policies to promote "cultural production, sustainable development associated with these practices, which, in order to survive, have to be profitable." His thoughts resonated with the exhibition on ICH and sustainable development displayed on the UNESCO headquarter fences and shown in digital form in the lobby of the hotel where we would spend the week following the work of the Committee.[19] This exposition included photographs illustrating how ICH can contribute to economic development, health, food security, environmental sustainability, social cohesion, and conflict prevention. It aimed to sensitize people to the recommendations formulated a few months earlier in the Chengdu International Conference on Intangible Cultural Heritage in Celebration of the Tenth Anniversary of UNESCO's Convention for the Safeguarding of the Intangible Cultural Heritage.[20]

While most elements since inscribed still pertain to festive and ritual events or performing arts, the influence of SD on the debates of the governing bodies of the Convention has led to an increasing number of listed practices that depart from what the NGO representative regarded as "folkloric" representations of ICH. They demonstrate how the SD narrative has influenced nominations and inscription decisions, where ICH is viewed less as fragile and threatened and more as a resource providing solutions to social, environmental, or economic issues. Most ICH elements, even the more conventional ones, are portrayed as contributors to the social dimension of SD through their creation and maintenance of social bonds among individuals and communities. Some of them, however, specifically embody particular knowledge and skills that have the potential to address risks associated with climate change or to establish particular relationships, valued as non-extractive, with the environment through controlled natural resource management.

Early examples include two projects submitted for inscription on the Representative List by Spain and Belgium respectively: the Irrigators' tribunals of the Spanish Mediterranean coast: the Council of Wise Men of the plain of Murcia and the Water Tribunal of the plain of Valencia, inscribed in 2009 and the Shrimp fishing on horseback in Oostduinkerke, inscribed in 2013. These practices are presented as environmentally respectful and socially regulated,

[19] https://ich.unesco.org/en/ich-for-sustainable-development-a-virtual-exhibition-2013-00693 (accessed November 11, 2023).

[20] ITH/13/EXP/8.

with the Water Tribunal applying customary law principles to resolve intracommunity conflicts related to common irrigation structures, and shrimp fishing relying on deep knowledge of the sea and shore, limited to three hours twice per week. A number of other practices relating to land or water management were inscribed in the following years, like the Traditional system of Corongo's water judges (Perou, 2017); the Knowledge and skills of the water measurers of the foggaras or water bailiffs of Touat and Tidikelt (Algeria, 2018); the Art of dry stone walling, knowledge, and techniques (Croatia, Cyprus, France, Greece, Italy, Slovenia, Spain and Switzerland, 2018); Al Aflaj, traditional irrigation network system in the UAE, oral traditions, knowledge and skills of construction, maintenance, and equitable water distribution (United Arab Emirates, 2020); and Traditional Irrigation in Europe: knowledge, technique and organization (Austria, Belgium, Germany, Italy, Luxembourg, The Netherlands, Switzerland, 2023).

Other practices consist of knowledge and skills related to natural resources and agro-pastoral practices, such as the Picking of Iva grass on Ozren mountain (Bosnia and Herzegovina, 2018); the Biocultural program for the safeguarding of the tradition of the Blessed Palm in Venezuela (Venezuela, 2019); Transhumance, the seasonal droving of livestock along migratory routes in the Mediterranean and in the Alps (Austria, Greece and Italy, 2019); Charfia fishing in the Kerkennah Islands (Tunisia, 2020); Ong Chun/Wangchuan/Wangkang ceremony, rituals, and related practices for maintaining the sustainable connection between man and the ocean (China and Malaysia, 2020); Tree beekeeping culture (Poland and Belarus, 2020); Beekeeping in Slovenia, a way of life (Slovenia, 2022); and Alpine pasture season (Switzerland, 2023).

Further examples focus on health, such as Acupuncture and moxibustion of traditional Chinese medicine (China, 2010); the Lum medicinal bathing of Sowa Rigpa, knowledge and practices concerning life, health, and illness prevention and treatment among the Tibetan people in China (China, 2018); Safeguarding foster care heritage in the merciful city of Geel: a community-based care model (Belgium, 2023); Midwifery: knowledge, skills and practices (Colombia, Cyprus, Germany, Kyrgyz Republic, Luxembourg, Nigeria, Slovenia, Togo, 2023); or Jamu Wellness Culture (Indonesia, 2023). Some inscribed elements instead consist of alternative social models, such as Idea and practice of organizing shared interests in cooperatives (Germany, 2016); involve risk prevention techniques such as the Avalanche risk management (Switzerland and Austria, 2018); or relate to conflict resolution like the Safeguarding strategy of traditional crafts for peace building (Colombia, 2019).

The UNESCO secretariat's emphasis on a SD-related understanding of ICH is evident in a visual representation of the ICH items inscribed on the lists of the

Convention. In 2019, the Secretariat developed an interactive online tool, Dive into Intangible Cultural Heritage,[21] to illustrate the interconnections between the elements inscribed on the lists. This was complemented by another tool, Dive into Living Heritage and Sustainable Development,[22] where correlations between the elements and the SDGs were visualized in relationship bundles based on information from the nomination files submitted by States Parties.

The official responsible for developing this tool views it as "a way of showing the diversity and scope of these fields and the complexity and multiple interpretations that can be made of them." From his perspective, it allows to emphasize how ICH "resonates" with SD (especially in terms of social cohesion) and, in particular, SDG 4 on quality education, as "all the elements of ICH can be involved, because ICH transmission is based on education." This tool was selected as one of UNESCO's projects to be presented during an event on Culture and Sustainable Development, organized in partnership between the UN General Assembly and UNESCO. Triggering representations of heritage through the prism of the SDGs, Dive into Living Heritage and Sustainable Development is meant to demonstrate how ICH can be "an accelerator of SDGs implementation,"[23] showcasing its ability "to drive social inclusion, poverty eradication, responsible environmental stewardship, sustainable economic growth, and ownership of development processes."[24]

1.3 Emulation Effect and Bureaucratic Agency

As manifestations of the international "authorized heritage discourse" (Smith, 2006), inscriptions on the lists established by the Convention spark an emulation effect. Within national heritage administrations, these perspectives on ICH lead to new developments in policy-making and the design of heritage programs and interventions. In turn, these projects may evolve into new nominations for the international lists of the Convention, further nurturing a shift toward understandings of ICH in relation to SD.

For instance, during a lunch organized at the margins of the Committee meeting held in Bogota in 2019, a discussion on the nomination of Dry Stone walling, which Luxembourg and Ireland were considering joining, prompted the Greek delegate to explain that their ICH policy was undergoing a shift: while

21 https://ich.unesco.org/en/dive&display=constellation#tabs (accessed September 13, 2023).

22 https://ich.unesco.org/en/dive&display=sdg#tabs (accessed September 13, 2023).

23 www.un.org/pga/75/2021/04/28/high-level-event-on-culture-and-sustainable-development-2/ (accessed September 13, 2023).

24 https://ich.unesco.org/en/news/21-may-the-united-nations-general-assembly-and-unesco-partner-for-an-event-during-the-world-day-for-cultural-diversity-for-dialogue-and-development-13308 (accessed September 13, 2023).

in previous years the focus had been on capacity-building workshops to promote the bottom-up rationale of the Convention, the primary objective was now sustainable development. The emphasis was, she explained, on understanding ICH as a means to cope with and mitigate climate change, as evidenced by projects like the dry stone walling and a recent one on transhumance, inscribed that same year. Similarly, a French official in charge of ICH, speaking at a conference in 2018, highlighted the inclusion of new kinds of items in the national inventory, such as construction techniques, irrigation, fishing, and agro-pastoral practices (Chave, 2021: 12).

Sustainable development similarly plays a crucial role in Swiss ICH policies (Vuilleumier and Hertz, 2024). The Federal Office for Culture aims, in fact, to guide cantonal approaches to ICH selection, stressing integration with SD. A new criterion, "contribution to sustainable development," was introduced for new items to be included in the national inventory ("List of Living Traditions in Switzerland"[25]). Moreover, the funding scheme established by the Federal Office for Culture for safeguarding projects prioritizes those focusing on SD, practically making the latter a thematic priority. The argument presented by the FOC is that:

> Living traditions are closely linked to sustainable development. Intangible cultural heritage enables the implementation of sustainability-oriented actions and solutions that promote living together. In this respect, it can make a significant contribution to the management of social and environmental challenges.[26]

The Swiss civil servant overseeing the implementation of the ICH Convention noted, in fact, that the country has the "good student syndrome," closely aligning its ICH safeguarding policies with the principles advocated by the Convention. As he explained, "the first elements nominated by Switzerland were festive events, then came the avalanche risks management, alpinism, also linked to SD, the alpine pasture season, and the *bisses* [i.e. traditional irrigation]." The "political project" driving this shift was that of "moving away from a traditionalist vision to highlight other contributions to society." This, in his view, showed that "choosing to focus on environmental elements is a way of moving away from this conservative, patriotic, reactionary vision."

In certain contexts, such as those mentioned earlier, SD priorities seamlessly combine with domestic policies, with countries leveraging the Convention as an additional source of legitimation. : In these cases, nominations for the ICH lists

[25] See www.lebendige-traditionen.ch/tradition/en/home.html (accessed September 13, 2023).

[26] See www.bak.admin.ch/bak/fr/home/actualites/nsb-news.msg-id-89943.html (My translation) (accessed September 13, 2023).

simultaneously align with international directives and comply with national priorities. Framing ICH safeguarding in terms of SD is seen here as a commitment to the fundamental mission of the heritage enterprise. As the Swiss official put it, “The basic question is what’s the point of safeguarding ICH? That’s where sustainability makes sense.”

Though, as had already become clear during the GA debate on the adoption a new chapter of the ODs focusing on SD, not all states are so enthusiastic about the establishment of a strong interrelation between ICH and SD (Jacobs 2024). As noted also by Smeets (2024: 46), the eager support of the European countries for this chapter was counterbalanced by the reservations of the Latin American and Asian nations and the silence of the African States Parties. Brazil, supported by Latin American and Caribbean states, as well as by India and China, claimed that it would be better to avoid “creative language” and adopt a more “sober” and “flexible” one, not “going too far”; namely, use the modal verb “shall” instead of “should” to dictate the mode of action. To illustrate his argument, the Brazilian delegate explained: “When I prepare a file on Capoeira I am not going to solve all issues regarding education, health etc. in a given community.” The Venezuelan delegate further stressed this point arguing that “other UN body deal with these issues much better. These have nothing to do with this institution’s specificity. We may create a risk for the Convention if we do not keep in mind that this is a Convention about culture.” The Ecuadorian delegation added, “We do not like the word security in this Convention. Is UNESCO going to be wearing helmets? UNESCO should focus on heritage!”

The bureaucratic apparatus of the Convention is, however, designed to trigger a SD-focused approach and to accordingly orient national ICH policies, even when such a safeguarding strategy is not already a priority in the first place. An audit mechanism, detailed in the final chapter, was established with the aim of prompting a more explicit understanding of ICH as being intertwined with SD. Moreover, a change made to the nomination form for the Representative List, effective since 2023, explicitly requests information on the nominated element’s contribution to SD. In fact, for the first two decades of the implementation of the Convention, reference to SD in the nomination file was usually simply intended to reflect the definition of ICH, which includes “compatibility” with SD. Furthermore, in explaining how the viability of a given cultural expression was to be ensured, the safeguarding measures described in the nomination file, such as in the aforementioned examples, often implied references to sustainability. This, however, was neither an explicit mention nor elicited by formal requirements formulated at the international level and translated in the bureaucratic apparatus of the Convention. Indeed, the criteria for inclusion on the international lists, reflected in the structure of the form, did not overtly focus on SD (UNESCO, 2020: 27–29).

A reflection on the function of the Convention's lists, organized by the UNESCO Living Heritage Entity[27] between 2021 and 2022, highlighted the need to make SD references explicit in the criteria for evaluating future nominations. This resulted in modifications to the form used for describing the element and justifying the request for inscription on the list.[28] The title of the section related to Criterion 2[29] was modified from "Contribution to ensuring visibility and awareness and to encouraging dialogue" to "Contribution to visibility, awareness, dialogue, *and sustainable development*" (emphasis added). The instructions provided in the nomination form on how to meet Criterion 2 were accordingly expanded: "States are encouraged, with reference to Chapter VI of the Operational Directives, to recognize the interdependence between the safeguarding of intangible cultural heritage and sustainable development." To explicitly illustrate this interdependence, the form introduces a new question asking whether the "communities concerned" believe that the submitted element contributes to one or more SD-related fields outlined in Chapter VI of the OD, namely food security, health care, quality education, gender equality, inclusive economic development, environmental sustainability, including climate change, and peace or social cohesion.

The above shows how the SD turn in the Convention is pragmatically channeled through the administrative tools employed in heritage production: an example of the agency and creativity of bureaucracy (Hull, 2012; Bortolotto et al., 2020). Indeed, the form explicitly emphasizes the role of SD and thereby molds specific representations of ICH. In the words of a former secretary of the Convention, this is how "the Convention's reset has started affecting listing mechanisms as well" (Smeets, 2024: 49).

An official of the French Ministry of Culture involved in preparing the nomination file for "The Skills of Parisian Roofers and Ornamentalists," acknowledged this influence while discussing the new form and the necessity to identify SD-related aspects of the know-how. She found this process intriguing, stating, "this is very interesting because it forces us to confront ourselves

[27] This section of the UNESCO Secretariat ensures the implementation of the Convention at the international level on a day-to-day basis and assists the statutory organs of the Convention.

[28] A new OD (39.2.b) also stipulates that states demonstrate the contribution to SD when requesting the transfer of an element from the Urgent Safeguarding List to the Representative List.

[29] "Inscription of the element will contribute to ensuring visibility and awareness of the significance of the intangible cultural heritage and to encouraging dialogue, thus reflecting cultural diversity worldwide and testifying to human creativity" (UNESCO, 2020: 28).

with sustainable development." She explained that they decided to tick two boxes: quality education and environmental sustainability. Regarding the former, she highlighted the updated training of roofers and ornamentalists, which incorporates technological innovation. For the latter, she emphasized the recycling of old zinc and the creative use of offcuts to minimize waste. Additionally, she underscored the development of new skills for installing glass wool, contributing to thermal isolation and reduced energy consumption.

While the full effects of these changes to the nomination form are yet to be observed and assessed, the requirement that new projects demonstrate their contribution to SD suggests that elements submitted for inscription on the Representative List will likely be chosen to substantiate this contribution. Notably, this emphasis on SD aligns with the prospective nature of ICH safeguarding and its potential as a catalyst for change. In this way, UNESCO is shaping particular representations of heritage, seen as an agent for change, through bureaucratic devices that have practical impact on the making of ICH locally (Bortolotto, 2020b).

2 Intangible Cultural Heritage as an Object *for* Change

The UNESCO narrative presenting SD as being "at the heart of the Convention" is part of a strategic and discursive process of "reorientation" (Smeets, 2024) intended to align the UNESCO programs with UN priorities and agenda. Emphasizing the fact that "the notion of 'sustainability' in the 2030 Agenda for Sustainable Development echoes the concept of 'living heritage' in the 2003 Convention for the Safeguarding of the Intangible Cultural Heritage,"[30] this narrative, however, also reflects the fact that safeguarding ICH, the key purpose of the Convention, actually intertwines with the objectives of what is conventionally called SD. In fact, safeguarding ICH boils down to the effort of keeping available and projecting *into the future* particular ways of strengthening social bonds, sustaining livelihoods, interacting with the environment and exploiting natural resources. I argue that the interrelation between ICH and SD can be conceptually approached and more fully understood by considering the particular temporality that underpins the idea of safeguarding, as opposed to conservation.

In articulating present needs with representations of the past and projects for the future, heritage can be regarded as a "machine for manipulating time" (Fabre, 2013: 58).[31] It reflects the kind of relationship that we have with cultural

[30] https://ich.unesco.org/en/sustainable-development-and-living-heritage (accessed September 13, 2023).

[31] My translation.

transmission and the social and political functions that we ascribe to it (Hartog, 2003: 166). Developed from European conservation and restauration paradigms (defined in the 1930s and 1960s respectively by the Athens and Venice Charters),[32] the Western understandings of heritage that have shaped international heritage policies and have been authorized at the global scale by UNESCO conceive heritage as a survival of the past to be cherished and preserved in its authenticity "for future generations," as the narrative goes (Harrison, 2020: 23). Even if a concern for the future underpins the rationale of the heritage mission, since the ultimate aim of heritage conservation has been conceptualized as a way of "perpetuating 'things' (. . .) into more or less distant futures" (Harrison et al., 2020: 4), heritage work is classically meant to establish a "communion" with the past (Voisenat, 2016: 30), what Meskell describes as a form of "past mastering" or "the struggle to come to terms with the past" (Meskell, 2012: 1). Heritage is, in sum, what "reminds people of the past" (Holtorf and Högberg, 2021: 2), its memory crystallized, embodied, and celebrated in particular places that become the symbol of a bygone world (Nora, 1997). This is why nostalgia has been regarded as a key concept for understanding heritage as a social phenomenon (Herzfeld, 2005; Berliner, 2012) and why heritage has been contested as a reactionary tool that values conservation over creation, the "beauty of the dead" (de Certeau et al., 1970) over the disturbing complexity of life.

Qualified by Lowenthal (Lowenthal, 1998: x) as "a profession of faith in a past tailored to present-day purposes," heritage is of course always produced in the present for present ends, what has been referred to as "presentism" (Hartog, 2003), "presentness of heritage" (Harvey, 2001: 321), or "past presencing" (Macdonald, 2013: 233).[33] However, even if we create heritage in the present, we give a second life (Kirshenblatt-Gimblett, 1998) to what is perceived as fading away, as no longer integrated into social life or used in its original function and being still subject to change. Indeed, as opposed to "history time," "heritage time" is subject to "arrested change" (Brumann, 2021: 268).

[32] The Athens Charter for the Restoration of Historic Monuments (1931) and the International Charter for the Conservation and Restoration of Monuments and Sites (ICOMOS, 1964).

[33] From a social sciences perspective, heritage is to be understood as a "verb" rather than as a "noun," not as a corpus of items but a social and political phenomenon (Harvey, 2001: 327). In other words, qualifying an object, site, or practice as "heritage" is not simply a description – as if the heritage value were already there, intrinsic to the object – transmitted from the past. Rather, it's a way of intervening in the status of that object and assigning it a value. This value is produced in the present and defined by contemporary needs and criteria. In this perspective, heritage is a claim. It singularizes particular items and, making their cultural value explicit, transforms them into cultural and identity symbols.

As the premise of the heritage enterprise, conservation ensures that change is arrested and heritage is transmitted to future generations.[34] However, the notion of conservation, embraced by the World Heritage Convention, is excluded by the ICH Convention and substituted with the concept of "safeguarding," intended as a set of "measures aimed at *ensuring the viability* of the intangible cultural heritage" (UNESCO, 2003, art. 2.3, my emphasis). Viability, in this context, refers to the ability to continue existing, developing, functioning adequately, and sustaining itself in changing social and historical contexts. ICH is therefore not meant to be conserved in its pristine form. It is instead a project to be developed. Its safeguarding is not about restoring or preserving what belongs to the past in order to benefit from it in the present but of projecting it into the future at the cost of its transformation. It is therefore the potential of ICH to bring about change, rather than reproduce sameness, and the centrality of the future in this process that incorporates the idea of sustainability in the ICH apparatus.

In sum, the concept of safeguarding introduces a *paradoxical* temporality into the heritage sphere, connecting it with new concerns and serving as a dynamic process for transmitting specific knowledge, skills, and social practices as renewed resources with functions consistent with ever-evolving contexts. The shift from conservation to safeguarding represents a significant paradigm change (Bortolotto, 2011) essentially altering the temporal regime of heritage and making the future, rather than the past, the key reference. This concept is embedded in the official UNESCO rhetoric. For instance, as early as 2002, Koïchiro Matsuura, director-general of UNESCO, stated that "[i]ntangible cultural heritage is not just the memory of past cultures, but is also a laboratory for inventing the future" (UNESCO, 2002).

It is, however, not this kind of discursive evidence that allows us to comprehend how, in practice, the ICH apparatus works as a laboratory for inventing the future. UNESCO operationalizes this temporality shift through practical means, translating this idea into a set of administrative devices.

2.1 Pigeonholing

The notion of ICH as a laboratory for reinventing the future, rather than a tool for maintaining continuity with the past, becomes clearer when examining the actual mechanisms and material tools involved in producing ICH, such as the nomination forms for inscription on the lists of the Convention. Far from being solely technical and administrative, these documents convey and channel a particular vision of ICH safeguarding.

34 Interestingly, the need to integrate change in tangible heritage conservation is called for when heritage is conceptualized as a resource for SD, particularly in a context of climate change (Holtorf, 2020).

To illustrate the performative impact of these bureaucratic tools on heritage representations, I draw from my experience as a "facilitator," coached by the UNESCO secretariat to offer "guidance and training for safeguarding intangible cultural heritage."[35] In 2012, the municipality of Pisa, Italy, was putting together a nomination of the city festival, called *Luminara*, for the Representative List and sought assistance in navigating UNESCO's forms and procedures. For a couple of years, I was involved in this project, working with the municipality, an anthropologist from Pisa University, and representatives from civil society organizations.

The Luminara festival commemorates San Ranieri, the city patron saint, every year on the 16th of June. It involves fixing ephemeral wooden structures to buildings in the historical city center, along the banks of the Arno River. These structures are usually attached to windows and support thousands of candles that are lit at sunset. People gather along the banks of the river to admire the effect of the lights. The result is regarded by the inhabitants as a "magical atmosphere," making them very proud of their belonging to the city, so much so that many people who have migrated to other parts of Italy or abroad travel back to their hometown for the occasion.

The process necessary for turning a cultural practice into a potential ICH element is an example of "soft guidance" (Larsen, 2013); namely, far from consisting of simple technical assistance, it has structuring effects. Here, I was an agent of this soft guidance and had the normative task of guiding my interlocutors in the preparation of the nomination form (called ICH-02) used for UNESCO-level evaluation, which any group seeking to inscribe their cultural practice on the Representative List must use.

This formatting proved frustrating for my counterparts as it restricted their ability to present their culture in the manner they desired. One participant expressed his exasperation, stating: "You're driving us crazy with this pigeonholing (*incasellamento*)." Indeed, the inputting of the information was perceived as "bureaucratic" procedure. This bureaucratization was particularly difficult to accept in drafting the section concerning the definition of the element, where the organizers of the Luminara wanted to express their attachment to this event, whereas I pushed them to describe their festival according to the UNESCO definition of ICH.

This process of pigeonholing the Luminara also had structuring effects in terms of local understandings of heritage temporality. It was in fact clear from the beginning that there were several divergences in how my counterparts understood the heritage value of the Luminara and UNESCO's perspective.

[35] https://ich.unesco.org/en/facilitator (accessed September 13, 2023).

For them, considering the Luminara as heritage entailed demonstrating how it was a survival from the past. Indeed, as soon as I arrived in Pisa, the first place I was brought was the archives. This was based on the assumption that evidence of the antiquity of the event was necessary for its recognition as heritage. Following the same rationale, I was subsequently given a pile of books on the history of the Luminara and introduced to elderly people and local historians who reassured me how little the contemporary event had changed over the years (since its beginnings in 1688). In essence, the focus was on the past and authenticity.

I had to tell the representatives of local authorities and civil society organizations that the form to present the Luminara for UNESCO evaluation had only a few lines available to describe the historical aspect of the element and that "authenticity" was a taboo concept for the evaluators (Deacon and Smeets, 2013; Bortolotto, 2020a). Instead, UNESCO expected explanation of how the practice had evolved over the years to remain meaningful and vital. Indeed, in order to prepare the nomination, we needed to work on so-called "safeguarding measures" addressing the "viability" of the Luminara.

Following numerous discussions among civil society organizations, the focus consequently shifted to the future of the Luminara in a changing social landscape characterized by new needs, such as adaptation to tourism growth and enhancement of security measures. Attention turned toward very concrete projects, such as recycling the plastic and aluminum of the cups supporting the candles used during the festival, developing "cultural tourism" through storytelling, and new urban planning extending the festival space with structures designed by international artists.

Although the project, submitted in 2014 and 2015 to the Italian National Commission for UNESCO, did not progress to the international stage,[36] notable here is not in the inscription itself but the transformative process that turned a cultural practice into an element of ICH to be potentially inscribed on such lists. This process induced a new perspective on the Luminara, future-oriented, centering on environmental, economic, and creative considerations. In other words, the need to align with UNESCO's form prompted a shift in local representations of heritage and of its transmission. The model of conservation of things past was replaced by that of safeguarding: heritage was no longer regarded as something to be preserved but as a project for the future. One that, in this case, involves less plastic and embraces resources from cultural tourism.

[36] States Parties to the ICH Convention can select one national project every two years for nomination for the UNESCO lists. The Art of Neapolitan "Pizzaiolo" was chosen in that period and inscribed in 2017.

2.2 Intangible Cultural Heritage Is Not Traditional

The example of the Luminara illustrates how, in practice, future becomes the time dimension shaping the ICH paradigm as designed by UNESCO. I argue that this orientation is specific to ICH. While "future-thinking" in heritage studies is seemingly beginning to move beyond the "axiomatic," "self-evident" motto of preserving the past for the future (Holtorf and Högberg, 2021: 1),[37] heritage is still often conceptualized in terms of the conservation of remnants from the past. If, as the UNESCO narrative goes, SD has always been "at the heart of the Convention," it is because ICH is operationalized as an *object for change*. Change lies at the core of the safeguarding concept, and with the rising importance of Sustainable Development as a rationale for safeguarding, this aspect is increasingly emphasized. Initially simply implicit, the contribution to SD is to be explicitly described and justified in new nominations to the Representative List. As seen in the Parisian roofers and ornamentalists example, this entails integrating new technologies and promoting innovation to address evolving needs in times of energy crises and climate change. Emphasizing the contribution of ICH to SD ultimately aims to highlight its potential for future exploitation of specific know-how rather than insisting on the reproduction of longstanding practices.

Observing debates within the governing bodies of the Convention provides additional evidence on this temporal shift and the importance placed on change and innovation. These aspects were openly underscored in discussions on SD, particularly in view of incorporating a new chapter into the ODs.[38] The Belgian delegate proposed deleting the adjective "traditional" before terms that, in the draft chapter, refer to domains of ICH, namely "farming," "healing," "health practices," "pedagogical methods," "water management systems," "knowledge about nature and universe," "knowledge of disaster risk reduction," "knowledge concerning the earth and climate," and so on. In proposing this amendment, he argued that "our central concept is not tradition but ICH," namely practices recognized by communities, groups, and individuals as contributing to their identity, irrespective of being primarily "traditional." A "norm entrepreneur" (Finnemore and Sikkink, 1998: 893) of this Convention, this delegate has often played a catalytic role, campaigning to introduce ideas and getting them

[37] This interest is grounded in a concern for the role and significance of heritage in the future, fostering a forward-looking perspective meant to proactively address challenges in managing heritage over the long term "in order to make better decisions on heritage and conservation in the present." Specifically, the idea is to consider "how future generations might relate to and be affected by heritage in different ways than we are today, requiring new ambitions for managing what today we call the historic environment" (Holtorf, 2022: 530–531).

[38] Specifically, during the 2015 session of the Intergovernmental Committee for the Safeguarding of the ICH.

accepted by a critical mass, to the point of their internalization as new norms. His normative intervention here highlights the evolving temporality of ICH, explicitly emphasizing non-past-oriented perspectives and the promotion of change and innovation within the official UNESCO discourse, particularly as SD becomes a core concept.

In the specialized understanding of folklorists and anthropologists, traditions are recognized as dynamic, constantly evolving entities that adapt to change (Lenclud, 1987; Phillips, 2004; Isnart and Testa, 2024). However, in common and political discourses, the concept of tradition often refers to practices rooted in the past – resisting modernity and innovation – seen as identity markers for specific groups. It is against this backward-looking understanding that the Belgian amendment sought to instead highlight the potential of ICH to play a dynamic role in societies, adapting to future needs or, to borrow his words, "transforming, not saving" (Jacobs and Neyrinck, 2020). This essentially illustrates how, if heritage is classically conceived as being about "manufacturing the past" (Meskell, 2018), UNESCO norm entrepreneurs rather seek to present ICH as a tool for manufacturing the future, thereby reflecting the actual uses of tradition observed on the ground in many different cultural contexts. Anthropological observations of these uses in fact stress that tradition is consciously mobilized for shaping "traditional futures" (Clifford, 2004), as a resource "for tomorrow" (Curtis, 2002: 239) that incorporates development into "ethno-futures" (Comaroff and Comaroff, 2009).

In this perspective, the temporality of heritage changes: the rationale of ICH safeguarding does not embody a responsibility toward the past, a duty of memory, but a responsibility towards the future. While past-oriented and nationalistic perspectives remain prevalent in many projects seeking inscription on the lists established by the Convention, the ICH paradigm, as it is intended in the doxa of the Convention and implemented through bureaucratic guidance, promotes a shift in the temporality of heritage that comes with new political and social functions. If classic heritage conservation was intended to resist change and ensure that future generations could represent themselves as coming from a particular past, ICH safeguarding has instead been conceived as having the potential to foster change and innovation. The goal is to equip future generations with tools and resources to navigate an increasingly uncertain and threatening future. In essence, UNESCO sees ICH not as a means for nostalgically retrieving the past to legitimize present projects but as a dynamic tool for envisioning and shaping possible futures.

This future- and change-oriented perspective increasingly underpins ICH-related initiatives on the ground. For instance, on the occasion of the twentieth anniversary of the ICH Convention an event was organized in Italy bringing together several partners from neighboring countries (Switzerland, Slovenia, France, and Austria). These nations had been working together for almost a decade on several projects aimed at promoting the Alpine Diet and were now seeking its international recognition through its inclusion on the UNESCO Register of Good Safeguarding Practices. Significantly, the title chosen for the event was "Sow the future, harvest communities."[39] The coordinators explained that this choice reflected the idea of the workshop circulating experiences, regarded as good practices able to inspire other collective projects offering opportunities for exploiting the social and economic dimensions of traditional knowledge. Indeed, the young farmers, bakers, winemakers, and shepherds intervening during the workshop were especially interested in the potential of the Alpine Diet to enhance their livelihoods and in building a model of development based on what was presented as a balanced exploitation of natural resources.

The perspective here is not that of conservative nostalgia. Knowledge and skills transmitted from generation to generation spur the same kind of feeling that Angé and Berliner have qualified as "eco-nostalgia," where "longings for past forms of life" are supposed to trigger forms of creativity that are "anything but traditional" (Angé and Berliner, 2020: 3). ICH, biosphere reserves, and biodiversity repositories such as the Svalbard Global Seed Vault are seen as "'de-extinction' initiatives" (Breithoff and Harrison, 2020: 101) and fields for experimenting and keeping available alternatives "envisioned as models for the future" (Bargheer, 2016: 123).

ICH, similar to genetic conservation, is positioned as a tool to address future threats. Here, the safeguarding of ICH provides possible alternatives for caring, managing natural resources, and sustaining livelihoods in the Anthropocene. Rooted in cultural practices transmitted "from generation to generation," often within indigenous, rural, or minority social contexts, these alternatives are perceived as solutions that, having proved effective in specific sociocultural contexts, can challenge the linear narrative of progress.

3 The Sustainabilization of Heritage

As a social phenomenon, heritage is circumstantial and evolving, shaped by particular historical, political, and cultural contexts. In other words, our representations of heritage, intended as "what we care about" (Tornatore, 2014), shift in response to changing political and societal priorities. The sustainabilization[40]

---

[39] *Seminare futuro, raccogliere comunità*, Milan, Lombardy Region, November 9, 2023.

[40] This concept is inspired by that of "climatization" (Aykut et al., 2017), defined as "a powerful yet uneven social process in which climate change is increasingly becoming the frame of reference for the mediation and hierarchization of other global issues" (Aykut and Maertens, 2021: 502).

of ICH, namely the process through which SD becomes the frame of reference for ICH governance and reshapes implicit or explicit criteria for defining safeguarding policies, is the most recent of these responses. This process is marked by a growing emphasis on what the UNESCO discourse refers to as the "intersectoral" potential of ICH, enabling it to play a role in what, it is claimed, are "the real articulations with the serious things that impact our lives," to borrow the words of a former secretary of the Convention. She also referred to "serious things" as "the hard aspects of society" extending beyond cultural sectors and policy fields, including health, the environment, and economics, as well as encompassing conflict resolution, emergencies, and crisis situations.

This focus on "intersectoriality," a key concept in the Sustainable Development vocabulary (Trowbridge et al., 2022), has been actively advocated by the secretariat since the initial efforts to integrate SD into ICH. The exhibition "Intangible Cultural Heritage for Sustainable Development," organized by the Convention's Secretariat in 2013 on the treaty's tenth anniversary, chose to highlight six key fields to illustrate the potential of ICH to address current social and political concerns. These included contributing to food security, strengthening social cohesion, respecting a sustainable environment, maintaining good health, sustaining livelihoods, and resolving disputes.[41]

The examples associated with each theme aimed to underscore the role played by ICH in the daily lives of people globally. For instance, the traditional foodways and local resource knowledge of the Isukha people in western Kenya are presented as enabling them to "be self-sufficient and live in harmony with their environment, fulfilling their needs." Frevo parades in Recife, Brazil, are depicted as bringing together people from diverse social strata, "giving them a sense of identity and strengthening community values that transcend differences of gender, ethnicity, class, and locality." The environmental knowledge required for mat weaving in Samoa is portrayed as a skill helping them "preserve their environment, recognizing that much of their well-being depends on nature." An Egyptian healing technique, involving burying patients in hot sand up to the waist for fifteen minutes, is showcased as a method for treating bone and joint diseases. Meanwhile, the practices of Estonian farmers who raise sheep and process their wool are presented as providing them "with a source of livelihood and identity," while also preserving "local handicraft traditions." The Water Tribunals of Valencia and Murcia serve as an illustration of resolving disputes over the scarce resource of water used for irrigation through verdicts "known to be equitable and wise, having the legal validity of any other civil court."

[41] https://ich.unesco.org/en/ich-for-sustainable-development-a-virtual-exhibition-2013-00693 (accessed November 11, 2023).

This approach of more explicitly underscoring the role of ICH in sectors traditionally seen as "non-cultural" would later form the basis of the new chapter of the ODs on ICH and Sustainable Development. Here, the secretariat explained, "the idea was to show that the safeguarding of intangible cultural heritage was not just an act of cultural preservation, but that this cultural dimension had an impact on health, environmental management, human rights, gender equality, and so on; dimensions that were part of the agenda for sustainable development."[42] In expressing her pride in the inclusion of a new chapter on ICH and SD in the ODs, the Secretary of the Convention at the time of these debates further underscored this concept: "It is really my vision of what ICH is *for* in life. ICH is *for* the environment, *for* health, *for* agriculture, *for* peace, *for* many things outside of the heritage box."(Duvelle et al., 2017: 31, my emphasis). In essence, UNESCO is establishing a new framework based on the imperative of "rethinking heritage for sustainable development," as articulated by Labadi (2022). Within this context, safeguarding ICH is not an end in itself; instead, it becomes a means to address other concerns deemed crucial to the future of humanity.

The assertion that the safeguarding of ICH is "essential if communities around the globe are ever to realize the future we want for all" in the brochure on ICH and SD, together with the incorporation of the new chapter in the ODs, reiterates the idea that fine-grained knowledge of the natural environment passed down through generations can serve as a resource for nutrition, food security, conservation of biological diversity, forest preservation, natural disaster prevention, or climate change adaptation. It further underscores that traditional therapeutic knowledge, including herbalism, can complement or serve as an alternative to biomedicine when other healthcare options are unavailable for treating physical or mental illnesses. It highlights that water management systems offer solutions to environmental challenges; social and festive events provide opportunities to strengthen social cohesion; and activities such as farming, pastoralism, fisheries, craftsmanship, and "ethical and ICH-sensitive" tourism can serve as sources of income. Finally, the brochure emphasizes that traditional mechanisms for conflict resolution and dialogue can be instrumental in achieving reconciliation.[43]

While presenting a somewhat idealized view of heritage that lacks the complexities of real-life situations, where heritage recognition can often have unintended or even counterproductive effects, such as fueling conflict instead of

[42] ITH/15/10.COM/4: 80.

[43] *Intangible Cultural Heritage and Sustainable Development* [online], https://ich.unesco.org/doc/src/34299-EN.pdf (accessed September 13, 2023).

promoting peace (Aykan, 2015), this perspective nonetheless underscores a new focus on the potential of ICH to offer solutions to contemporary anxieties. In this context, the knowledge passed down from previous generations is seen as a valuable resource for coping with uncertainty and crisis, perceived not only as a disrupting event but also as a chronicized phenomenon of instability (Masco, 2017) or as a structural mutation into the Antropocene (Stengers, 2009; Latour, 2017).

3.1 Intangible Cultural Heritage for Crisis

ICH in crisis situations has been a topic of discussion within the governing bodies of the Convention since 2016. Debates have highlighted the dual nature of intangible cultural heritage, portraying ICH respectively as threatened, fragile, and in need of protection and as a resource to be leveraged in emergency situations. In 2019, during a debate on the "Operational principles and modalities for safeguarding intangible cultural heritage in emergencies," the Committee specifically emphasized the potential of ICH as a resource during crisis. Various facets of "emergency" were explored by Committee members, including the displacement of people, climate change, natural hazards, political turmoil, post-conflict situations, and terrorism. Some states argued for expanding the concept of crisis to embrace the 2030 Agenda. Austria, for example, pointed out that "there are not only natural disasters and armed conflicts. There are also the effects of climate change reflected in slow decay and deterioration." This situation was illustrated and emphasized by the Netherlands, with a concrete example from Curacao, a Caribbean Island in the Kingdom of the Netherlands regularly affected by hurricanes, intensified by climate change. In such situations, it was suggested that humanitarian interventions could incorporate an "ICH perspective into their work." The Philippines stressed the role of ICH in these situations and advocated for a "more intersectoral approach," emphasizing that "communities have the capacity to reduce risks by drawing on their ICH."

Certain states, such as Palestine, Azerbaijan, and Cyprus, suggested that ICH can serve as a valuable resource for displaced communities, including internally displaced persons and refugees. The social function of ICH for recovering from natural disaster and reviving a sense of belonging was emphasized by Japan, with reference to the earthquakes and tsunami that had recently hit the country. Here, the Japanese delegate explained, performing arts and festivals provide displaced people with opportunities for social gatherings and community building. This social function was emphasized as an important resource in a context of peace building and reconciliation by Colombia with specific reference to the project "Safeguarding strategy of traditional crafts for peace building," which had recently been included in the Register of Good safeguarding Practices.[44] Building on the perspective of the Colombian delegate, Senegal highlighted the potential of ICH to consolidate peace. They referred in particular to the joking relationships inscribed on the Representative List by Niger. The Senegalese delegate meanwhile argued that this practice serves as a form of social regulation, facilitating dialogue and helping to initiate the first peace meetings in the context of the terrorist crisis in the Sahel.

During the December 2019 debate, no one mentioned pandemics as a source of crisis. Though, when COVID-19 suddenly emerged just a few months after this meeting, causing global lockdowns, the UNESCO secretariat initiated a survey on living heritage experiences during the pandemic.[45] Some of these experiences revealed that the transmission of ICH had shifted to online platforms. Examples include the Popayán processions in Colombia and Corpus Christi celebrations in Panama. In France, *Fest-noz*, a festive gathering centered around traditional Breton dances, underwent a transformation with the introduction of home-delivered gavotte. A *Fest-noz* practitioner noted that these changes were particularly challenging given that this collective activity, rooted in proximity and human warmth, embodied the very "antithesis of social distancing." [46]

Other experiences illustrate how ICH could help mitigate some of the consequences of the pandemic. Carrillions rang in Belgian and Northern French towns to provide moral support to the population and foster social cohesion – a goal aligned with the project "Safeguarding the carillon culture: preservation, transmission, exchange and awareness-raising" included in the Register of Good Safeguarding Practices in 2014. Other cases highlighted how ICH could contribute to preventing the spread of the virus by transmitting essential public health messages. For instance, a master of Chapei Dang

[44] During the workshop "Intangible Cultural Heritage and Emergencies: Prevent, Resist and Reconcile" organized in 2022 by the Centre français du patrimoine culturel immatériel (CFPCI) in partnership with the UNESCO Chair "Intangible cultural heritage and sustainable development," a representative from a Colombian NGO explained that these centers have become inclusive spaces that offer dialogue opportunities to victims, former combatants, apprentices, masters, and various marginalized groups. This includes individuals affected by the conflict, demobilized members of armed groups struggling to find employment, those displaced by violence, women supporting households, ethnic minorities, and people with disabilities.

[45] https://ich.unesco.org/en/living-heritage-and-the-covid-19-pandemic-01179 (accessed December 20, 2023).

[46] Julie Léonard, Responsable des inventaires du PCI, Bretagne Culture Diversité *Le fest-noz au risque de la covid-19 : entre adaptation et résistance / The fest-noz at the risk of covid-19: between adaptation and resistance (Vitré collloque crises).*

Veng, a Cambodian musical tradition inscribed on the Urgent Safeguarding List in 2016, sang about hand-washing, social distancing, and other COVID-19 safety measures. Examples from various continents highlight the manufacturing of face masks using traditional patterns, materials, and decorative techniques. A notable image featuring three Peruvian artists in folk costume wearing masks with "traditional patterns" was showcased on the Convention's website as an iconic representation of the role ICH can play during the pandemic. The artists' intention was to "optimistically show through art a way to identify with (. . .) native culture in these difficult times of the pandemic and spread Sarhuino art (. . .) In addition, being a venture that will provide financial support to Sarhuina families during the emergency."

Just as COVID restrictions were lifted in many regions, a war began in the heart of Europe. The Living heritage entity organized a coordination meeting to assess the needs of Ukrainian displaced communities in neighboring countries and to evaluate the potential of ICH to deal with the emotional, psychological, social, and economic distress caused by displacement in a situation of armed conflict. Previous UNESCO-led projects had likewise focused on the role of ICH in contexts of forced displacement both in the North Kivu region (Democratic Republic of Congo)[47] and among the displaced Syrian population.[48] These projects aimed to improve the living conditions of displaced people and contribute to strengthening the social bonds between refugees and host communities. Several projects were initiated by civil society organizations both within and outside Ukrainian borders. For instance, the network of NGOs accredited to the Convention launched a social media campaign (#livingheritageforpeace and #ICHpysankyforpeace) inspired by the Ukrainian tradition of decorating Easter eggs, known as pysanky, which symbolize new life, hope, and protection against evil. Workshops for decorating eggs aimed to facilitate the integration of the newly arrived Ukrainian refugees in various European countries and to strengthen social bonds with host communities, utilizing ICH as "powerful tool for peace-building and enhancing intercultural dialogue and resilience."[49]

---

[47] *Identification des besoins de sauvegarde du patrimoine culturel immatériel avec la participation des communautés dans la région du Nord-Kivu, République démocratique du Congo*. Rapport final. Préparé pour la Section du patrimoine culturel immatériel de l'UNESCO par Géraldine Chatelard. Avec la contribution de René Bitangi Mikombe, Richard Kambale Matsipa, Blandine Masemo Zaina et Anifa Safi Vahavi. Décembre 2017. https://ich.unesco.org/fr/projets/identification-des-besoins-de-sauvegarde-du-patrimoine-culturel-immateriel-dans-le-nord-kivu-avec-la-participation-des-communautes-00378 (accessed December 20, 2023).

[48] *Intangible Cultural Heritage of Displaced Syrians*. Prepared for UNESCO's Intangible Cultural Heritage Section by Dr. Géraldine Chatelard with input from Ms. Hanan Kassab Hassan. November 2017. https://ich.unesco.org/doc/src/38275-EN.pdf (accessed December 20, 2023).

[49] www.ichngoforum.org/news/living-heritage-peace-social-media-initiative/ (accessed December 20, 2023).

UNESCO has advocated for the use of ICH to address crises, not only on a practical level but also symbolically, serving as a source of pride and support for populations affected by armed conflicts and emergency situations. In 2022, following the initial submission in March 2021 for inscription on the Representative List, Ukraine requested that the Committee examine the nomination "Culture of Ukrainian borscht cooking" for inscription on the Urgent Safeguarding List as a case of extreme urgency.[50] The Evaluation body recommended inscribing the element, acknowledging the threat to its viability "as people are unable not only to cook or grow local vegetables for borscht, but also to come together to practice the element, which undermines the social and cultural well-being of communities."[51] Simultaneously, the Evaluation Body recognized that the practice promotes social cohesion among Ukrainian people "by providing a sense of resilience and solidarity."[52] "We believe it is a victory of culture," commented the Ukrainian Minister of Culture in his zoom intervention following the inscription.

A few months prior, another soup had been inscribed on the Representative List, following an emergency procedure – the Joumou soup (2021). This pumpkin soup, made with vegetables, plantains, meat, pasta, and spices, is described in the nomination form as a source of pride and identity for the Haitian population. Originally reserved for slave owners, it was transformed by independent Haitians into "a symbol of their newly acquired freedom and an expression of their dignity and resilience."[53] In the wake of an earthquake and storm that struck the country in August 2021, coupled with broad social and political turmoil due to the assassination of the Haitian president, the inscription was intended to be a source of pride and hope for the people of Haiti as they sought to recover from these emergencies.[54]

In summary, ICH is conceptualized as a valuable resource for addressing various crises in our daily lives, ranging from the heightened risks of natural hazards induced by climate change to armed conflicts, displacement, and pandemics. ICH is depicted not only as a force that forges social bonds and unites communities but also, increasingly, as a repository of knowledge and

[50] As per Article 17.3 of the 2003 Convention. [51] LHE/22/17.COM 4.BUR/5: 46.

[52] LHE/22/5.EXT.COM/5: 2.

[53] Nomination file no. 01853 for inscription in 2021 on the Representative List of the Intangible Cultural Heritage of Humanity https://ich.unesco.org/en/RL/joumou-soup-01853 (accessed October 20, 2024).

[54] Ricarson Dorce. "La mobilisation de la soupe au giraumon en situation d'urgence," Presentation at the workshop "Patrimoine vivant en situation d'urgence," Vitré, Centre français du patrimoine culturel immatériel (CFPCI), November 17–18, 2022.

skills with the potential to help cope with apocalyptic scenarios involving water shortages, hunger, forced migration, and social and political upheaval.

3.2 Avalanche Risk Management

Avalanche risk management, nominated by Switzerland and Austria and inscribed on the UNESCO Representative List of Intangible Cultural Heritage in 2018, serves as an illustrative example of the sustainabilization of ICH. It demonstrates that the latter is no longer seen as limited to the realm of folk traditions such as dance, songs, and festivals and proves instead that the field of ICH is expanding to encompass empirical knowledge and practical strategies with pragmatic utility in everyday life, particularly within the context of climate change, such as local risk cultures.

The narrative of the official nomination underscores how avalanche risk management (ARM) has shaped the identity of Alpine populations "as they have to deal, every winter, with a threat that looms over the heads of inhabitants, tourists, animals, means of communication and other infrastructure so vital for life in high lands."[55] On the one hand, the danger and the sense of solidarity created by the risk become a "source of identity" and traditional empirical knowledge of nature and the environment are conventionally presented as expressions of ICH. On the other hand, and significantly for my argument, the synergy between traditional skills developed over generations to manage avalanches and "methods developed through scientific knowledge," is highlighted as a combination "essential for addressing future challenges (e.g., climate change)." The complementary relationship between the local empirical knowledge of laypeople and technological development highlights the importance of peer learning and the ways that "knowledge is transferred from science to practice and from the ground to research."

The nomination accordingly provides a comprehensive and inclusive depiction of the "community concerned," devoid of romantic simplifications that might limit it to local mountain villagers familiar with the dangers of snow. In addition to "local players," predominantly consisting of volunteers like ski instructors, mountain guides, members of avalanche commissions, and security officers in ski resorts who constitute the network of observers of snow conditions, the community is presented as encompassing researchers and public authorities. It is also portrayed as involving civil society organizations focused on prevention, such as Alpine clubs or various mountain sports organizations

[55] Nomination file no. 001380 for inscription in 2018 on the Representative List of the Intangible Cultural Heritage of Humanity. https://ich.unesco.org/en/RL/avalanche-risk-management-01380 (accessed December 20, 2023).

offering courses to share experiences on ARM, as well as private companies developing rescue equipment and prevention devices.

The WSL Institute for Snow and Avalanche Research SLF, based in Davos, is described as a key constituent of the ARM community in Switzerland. At the forefront of research on snow, the atmosphere, natural hazards, permafrost, and mountain ecological systems, the institute utilizes sophisticated technical equipment such as remote sensing and cold and climatic chambers, with strong applied objectives. It develops various tools and products, including hazard maps, to make scientific knowledge accessible to the population in mountain environments, contributing to risk prevention. The institute also exchanges data and measurements with the Swiss Federal Office for Meteorology and Climatology and offers avalanche safety training programs. In describing their data collection methodology, scientists at the WSL emphasize the crucial role of the network of observers reporting on aspects of snow conditions that “you cannot easily measure” with remote sensing and technological devices. They explain that the information gathered “out there” by these observers includes “a lot of their feeling, their judgment” and that their feedback is crucial “to validate the predictions of our people in the institute.”

In explaining how the inscription of ARM would raise awareness on the importance of ICH in general, the nomination insists on how the latter will draw attention to the fact that “the know-how needed to move in a hostile environment pertains to ICH,” thus strengthening the linkages between the Convention and natural sciences. The nomination underscores that the prevention of natural hazards has a significant cultural dimension, and that a combination of various types of knowledge – traditional and empirical alongside modern and scientific – is essential for addressing future challenges.

The integration of lay knowledge,[56] traced back to the fifteenth century and transmitted through everyday experiences in the Alpine environment, with scientific research and technical innovation developed within an internationally recognized research center is here presented as a crucial argument to highlight the “originality” and relevance of this project. In developing an “integration narrative” common to other international arenas, such as climate conferences (Foyer and Dumoulin Kervran, 2017), ARM explicitly transfer in the ICH international regime the idea that local and “indigenous knowledge is more than merely traditional and local; it can contribute new data and perspectives to

[56] These observers, who have often played this role for several decades, are referred to as “*gents du cru*,” borrowing the expression used by the director of the Swiss Association of Mountain Guides.

modern science, and thus participate in designing innovative adaptation strategies" (Foyer and Dumoulin Kervran, 2017: 166).

This reflects a clear interest in integrating ICH and SD at the policy level. According to a former Swiss cultural heritage advisor, the rationale behind the choice of nominating ARM was to strategically showcase at the international level an image of Switzerland as being at the forefront of scientific research and technological innovation in this field. According to an FOC official, however, the shift from folklore to practices deeply embedded in practical aspects of everyday life, embracing prospective and "intersectoral" approaches, was a deliberate political choice going far beyond cultural diplomacy and ultimately seeking to "detach folklore from nationalism and highlight other contributions to society."

This initiative, in fact, emerged out of the scientific and political engagement of several ethnologists in charge of identifying elements for the Swiss national inventory. In departing from conventional understandings of ICH, their objective was to "show that this Convention is about more than carnival" and that their involvement with this instrument, far from trivial, could contribute to addressing crucial and concrete concerns of the population. In this context, focusing on environmental elements was primarily seen as a way to move away from a conservative, patriotic, and reactionary approach and, ultimately, to propose an alternative political role for heritage.

3.3 Safeguarding Foster Care Heritage in the Merciful City of Geel: A Community-Based Care Model

Included on the "Register of Good Safeguarding Practices" in 2023, "Safeguarding foster care heritage in the merciful city of Geel: a community-based care model" is described in the project submitted by Belgium as "an interesting form of contemporary psychiatric care which has a rich cultural tradition and remains an innovative and inspiring model for the future. It encourages social participation of mentally vulnerable people and destigmatizes mental illness".[57] The form submitted to UNESCO further explains that psychiatric family foster care revolves around a "healthcare community" composed of 135 foster families, the Geel society at large, and the Openbaar Psychiatrisch Zorgcentrum (Public Psychiatric Care Centre, hereafter OPZ) ensuring respectively care, room and board, inclusive integration, and a professional healthcare ecosystem.

[57] Nomination file no. 00622 for inscription in 2023 on the Register of Good Safeguarding Practices. [online] https://ich.unesco.org/en/BSP/safeguarding-foster-care-heritage-in-the-merciful-city-of-geel-a-community-based-care-model-00622 (accessed December 20, 2023).

This healthcare model is based on the principle that individuals with psychological vulnerabilities are not hospitalized and isolated from society. Instead, provided they possess sufficient social skills, they are hosted by a foster family and integrated into the everyday life of a community. While working and participating in social life, they are monitored by a multidisciplinary medical team. In the past, boarders mainly worked on the farms where they lived. Today, in a changed social and economic context, they engage in housekeeping, contribute in town workshops, participate in activities organized by the OPZ (such as a bicycle repair workshop, animal care, growing and selling vegetables), or volunteer in the Hospital museum or the OPZ visitor center.

The evolving socioeconomic models resulting from the shift from agriculture to industrialization and modernization in the region have led to a progressive decrease in the number of foster care families, highlighting the fragility of the Geel model and the challenges it faces.[58] In discussing the rationale for an information session for prospective foster families, a nurse and a social worker from the OPZ foster care team explained that they hoped to recruit more foster families as their number was rapidly decreasing (by twenty per year). They said that the desire to increase the number of these families was one of the reasons behind the application to the UNESCO Register.

"Radical acceptance," as explained by one of the project coordinators, defines the family foster care model. The nurse from the OPZ foster care team proudly emphasized that "when people come to Geel, they want to stay because it is very warm." In such a framework, she argued, there is "no need to change," and "for many people, this is a relief – to just be themselves, whereas at the hospital, they were under pressure to be cured." The emphasis on "care" rather than "therapy" is reflected in the fact, highlighted by the project coordinators, that these individuals are not called "patients" but "boarders," in an approach meant to accept them for who they are rather than attempting to "fix" them.

As proudly emphasized by the OPZ foster care team, a strategy based on tolerance and inclusiveness yields positive outcomes in terms of the health and well-being of the boarders. They argue that research conducted since the nineteenth century has demonstrated that such a system provides boarders with structure and autonomy, a sense of safety, and valorizes their potential. The integration into family and community life is said to allow for a reduction in reliance on pharmaceutical treatments. The health conditions of the boarders are regularly assessed by the OPZ foster care team, which comprises one social worker, six nurses (with specializations in psychiatrics and palliative care), four

[58] In 1986 the system could count on 743 foster families decreased to 455 in 1999 (Villa, 2020: 260). Families are supported with pubic funding in order to cover the living expenses generated by the borders.

psychiatrists, and two physicians. While the psychiatric hospital provides assistance when needed and ensures a bed is always available for the boarders, it plays a minimal role in their daily lives.

These advantages, according to the team, explain why academics and medical professionals come to Geel to study this model, which has inspired numerous initiatives globally. Preserved in the archives of the psychiatric hospital, a collection of professionals' cards left during the last century by psychiatrists from Europe, Japan, Brazil, the United States, and beyond provides evidence of the global interest in the Geel model. These points are emphasized in the form submitted to UNESCO and set forth as the rationale for considering it a good practice "inspirational for other communities and groups throughout the world." The nomination highlights, in particular, how Geel could serve as a model for developing countries with limited medical infrastructures and economic resources. Combining professional and voluntary work, this practice is presented as economically cost-effective compared to other institutional approaches.

Geel has, in fact, served as inspiration for several international projects. According to the project coordinators, the Geel experience catalyzed the establishment of an international research network (G.R.E.P.F.A., Groupe de Recherche Européen en Placement Familial) within the de-institutionalization movement around psychiatry in the 1980s, disseminating Psychiatric Family Foster Care across Europe. Reflecting on international experiences influenced by the Geel model, among which the better known is the Broadway Houses Communities project in New York, the curator of the Hospital Museum emphasized that while Psychiatric Family Foster Care elsewhere exists as a "project," in Geel it is simply "normal," integral to the social skills transmitted through generations within the Geel community or, to borrow the expression of the coordinators of the UNESCO project, "part of the DNA in Geel."

The Belgian project further elaborates on the cultural, as opposed to project nature of Psychiatric Family Foster Care in Geel, highlighting how its "values are everywhere: in policy plans, participatory projects, community life, and in the respectful language used in communication." This is why animated controversies have arisen over the potential removal of street signs reading "Attention family foster care," introduced in the 1950s due to increased traffic accidents involving boarders. While some view these signs as sparking curiosity and potentially stigmatizing the boarders as local attractions reminiscent of the nineteenth-century "colony of the mad," others see them as reflecting the full integration of Psychiatric Family Foster Care into local culture. The deep connection between the town and the Psychiatric Family Foster Care tradition is also evident in sports culture, with the local football team adopting slogans like "We are the fools from Geel" (Wij zijn de Geelse zotten) or "Zotten on Tour," (*i.e.* "the mad" *on Tour*), expressing pride in their role in shaping Geel's identity (Villa, 2020: 263).

The intergenerational transmission of foster care practices within households and the deeply embedded connection with the local community are explained as a rooted historical phenomenon. "It is the history that makes it possible for Geel," argued the OPZ foster care coordinator. Contemporary foster care practices are in fact intertwined with the legend of Saint Dympna,[59] the patroness of those suffering from nervous and mental disorders, whose cult has attracted pilgrims for 700 years. Initially hosted in the small hostel annexed to the church, these individuals were subsequently dispatched among local families. Over time, a hagio-therapeutic system where family foster care was organized by the clergy evolved, seeing the building of a psychiatric hospital in 1850 and eventually a scientifically and medically supported program coordinated by the psychiatric hospital.

The spiritual dimension of these traditions has not, however, been replaced by medical intervention. Although the novena rituals in which pilgrims, labeled as "possessed" or "mad," once engaged no longer exist, the vitality of the cult of St. Dympna is evident in prayers and chaplets dedicated to St. Dympna offered on Catholic websites for those "overwhelmed by anxieties." The pilgrimage to the church of Saint Dympna in Geel, where her relics are preserved, continues. The pilgrim book at the church collects prayers from believers in various languages, seeking St. Dympna's intercession in relieving family members and friends of depression, healing sons or daughters with mental health issues, intervening in situations of suicide contemplation, but also for people who need to "get off drugs," have "gender dysphoria," or "personality disorders." Some express gratitude to the Saint for helping them being "stable" and "calm."

Within this context, the Belgian nomination file argues that the epithet of the "Merciful City" is continually revitalized in the effort to "highlight the value of collaboration and complementarity among diverse healthcare approaches by nurturing a warm-hearted ecosystem where both cultural and healthcare practices (as living heritage) and medical institutions merge." Indeed, foster care has adapted to evolving representations of mental illness and changes in psychiatric therapies, particularly with the introduction of psychiatric drugs since the

[59] Legend has it that in the seventh century, Dymphna, an Irish princess, found refuge in Geel. Following her mother's death, her father's mental health declined, and he sought a new bride resembling his late wife. To escape his advances, Dymphna went to Geel, where she established a hospice for the poor and sick. Found by her father, she was beheaded by him in a fit of rage. In her honor, a church was built, attracting to her tomb pilgrims seeking treatment for psychiatric disorders.

1950s. Despite the need for constant medical oversight, this innovation has in fact facilitated smoother social integration of patients and transformed perceptions of mental illness (Villa, 2020).

3.4 The Past as Experience

Seeing healthcare practices or hazard risk management as expressions of ICH is described in the respective nomination files as having an "eyeopener effect" and as a crucial factor of "originality." The potential of these examples is, in both cases, highlighted in relationship to SD. The nomination of "Safeguarding foster care heritage in the merciful city of Geel: a community-based care model" argues that "Geel is an instructive case in understanding ICH in relation to sustainable development" and emphasizes how this healthcare model "strongly embodies the principles of contributing to achieving quality healthcare for all (SDG 3), and of OD179 on safeguarding ICH and sustainable development through healthcare." Similarly, Avalanche Risks Management is presented as being "essential for addressing future challenges (e.g., climate change) in a sustainable manner."

Both expressions refer to the possibility of expanding the field of ICH beyond its more conventional understanding, as generally reflected in the 730 elements now inscribed on the international lists.[60] Indeed, this shift in the understanding of heritage is not yet mainstream. Most common are folkloric and nationalistic approaches to ICH. Following the inclusion of ARM on the Swiss national inventory (in 2013), an article in the newspaper *Le Matin*, for instance, rhetorically asks whether a more "typical" example might have better represented Swiss identity and whether "avalanche risk management can really be regarded as a tradition." The journalist explains his understanding of what a tradition is supposed to be: "tradition should be felt in the gut and squeeze the heart at its mere evocation. It should have a popular side and build our collective imagination, whatever your political color. If you were abroad, wouldn't an evening of fondue and playing jass be more representative of your 'Swissness'?"[61] (Martino, 2014: 2).

In both of the projects described above, this essentializing discourse is carefully avoided. Emphasis on historical depth is never past-oriented but is instead viewed as a source of evolution. As the OPZ foster care team argued, "we are proud of the history and use of the history to progress nowadays." This perspective on pragmatic, rather than celebratory, uses of the past is expressed in the explanation given by the promoters of the UNESCO project when concern was raised within the OPZ board that "when you say the word

[60] As of October 2024. [61] My translation.

'heritage' in Flemish it means something dead, something from the past." Influenced by this understanding of heritage, the medical staff, in fact, regarded the recognition of Psychiatric Family Foster Care as heritage as a potentially hindering scientific innovation aimed at experimenting, updating, and "rethinking" the system (e.g., extending foster care to children as well). To counter this vision of heritage as past-oriented, the project promoters clarified that "the goal was not to conserve something from the past but that it was for the future and that changing it was very much part of the process." The historical depth of the family foster care is not seen in contradiction to its adaptation to contemporary and future challenges. Here, the practices of the past are more experiences to leverage than celebrations of identity. As the nurse of the OPZ foster care team observed, foster care in Geel "is something from the Middle Ages, and now it is a best practice."

This dynamic is particularly salient in the case of ARM. While the nomination highlights that knowledge about ARM has been transmitted since at least the fifteenth century, it also emphasizes its constant innovation and the role of technology in this process. For instance, the safeguarding measures include plans "to further develop new digital information solutions such as the mobile application www.whiterisk.ch." White Risk is a portal developed by WSL/SLF for avalanche prevention. A homonym application allows users to manage avalanche risks in the planning of a mountain tour through meteorologic data and avalanche bulletins. It is also through this application that observers can send information to WSL/SLF for the avalanches bulletin. This digital tool therefore plays an important role in the development of knowledge and of know-how on ARM. Furthermore, as noted by Severo and Vassor,[62] social media associated with White Risks have become the place where discussions about snow conditions and avalanche risks now occur. Here, the combination of institutional and professional knowledge with empirical wisdom exchanged among peers hybridizes scientific and practical knowledge based on everyday experience.

Rather than the nostalgia typical of Western and European outlooks on heritage (Berliner, 2012), what is emphasized in the above two examples are innovation and change, be it at the level of medical approaches and pharmacological therapies or that of natural-hazard related research and technology. ICH is understood here as knowledge and skills cultivated and refined across generations, where innovation is fully integrated.

[62] Marta Severo and Mathilde Vassor, ANR COLLABORA Création, documentation et valorisations collaboratives des cultures et des patrimoines (ANR-18-CE38-0005).

4 Diversity and Standardization

Increasingly framed as a reservoir of experiences cultivated across diverse cultures to address concrete problems of our times, social practices recognized as ICH provide alternative perspectives on understanding and experiencing the relationship with nature and the environment, healing and care, strengthening social bonds, and sustaining livelihoods. These encompass a wealth of insights accumulated over generations by collectives worldwide, transcending Western and capitalist modernity. The notion that the ecological wisdom of indigenous peoples serves as a sustainable interaction model with the broader environment is certainly a common cliché. And yet, from the perspective of the believers in the power of ICH, the latter potentially contributes to what Tsing describes as a "polyphony," where "autonomous melodies intertwine" in contrast to the "unified coordination of time" embodied by progress, thereby opening our imaginations to creative assemblages instead of adhering to standardized models of progress (Tsing, 2015: 23).

ICH embodies here the hope of contributing to what Gore and Moore refer to as "sustainable prosperity" (Moore, 2015: 808) and aligning with the shared anthropological view that a sustainable future relies on diversity in every domain (Carneiro da Cunha, 2017). For example, according to an active member of the network of NGOs accredited to the Convention, the realization that the diversity of ICH could be used as a creative resource for addressing real-world problems was an "aha-moment" for her organization – a moment of sudden insight that motivated her colleagues to engage with the UNESCO framework, previously viewed skeptically as reflective of normative, hegemonic, top-down, and neocolonialist perspectives on heritage and its societal functions.

Presented in the Convention as a "mainspring of cultural diversity," cultural and social practices falling under the purview of ICH are accordingly esteemed in the UNESCO narrative for their high potential to support a culture-centered approach to SD "against the mainstream, homogeneous, and universal model of development" (Wiktor-Mach, 2020: 321). At the same time, however, UNESCO complies with a management and audit culture (Strathern, 2000) that relies on technologies of standardization, presumed to guarantee effectiveness, reliability, and objectivity. These technologies organize cultural diversity within an established framework defined by a set of recognized criteria. In this process, particularism – intrinsically incommensurable – is rendered commensurable through its framing into formats and procedures, thus providing a common syntax to organize and arrange diversity (Bortolotto, 2014). It is this very process that transforms diversity into a resource with potential beyond its original circumscription. Yet, and paradoxically, this same process channels diversity into structures that mold it according to standard principles and criteria.

The tension between particularism and standardization became notably apparent when UNESCO engaged in the debate leading to Agenda 2030 at the UN level. In order to be heard, UNESCO was compelled to conceptualize culture within standard frameworks, namely the Sustainable Development Goals (SDGs), and in terms of measurable results. In other words, to actively participate in this process UNESCO had to align with the data-based approach to Sustainable Development employed by the UN. Former director-general Irina Bokova elucidated this challenge during a lecture on "Heritage for Sustainable Development,"[63] commenting:

> For a long time, we could not understand why our message was not accepted. In New York, where the diplomats were sitting, there was not a good understanding of why culture should be included in the sustainable development agenda. We did two big conferences in Hangzhou and in Florence and we confronted one problem: if you look at most SDGs, they have very specific targets that can be quantified. You can have a real sense of what is there. But culture is not something that you can easily quantify. The questions that we were asked were about measuring the impact of culture (. . .).

Adopting a quantitative approach to cultural policies was a strategic move by UNESCO in advocating for the inclusion of culture in the SDGs. This perspective allowed the Organization to assert that culture can play a tangible role in SD. The value attributed to culture, emphasized through this quantitative lens, aligned with the expectations of "diplomats sitting in New York," who were primarily acquainted with logics shaped outside the culture sector. To this regard, Irina Bokova noted in the aforementioned lecture:

> We prepared a report showing how much cultural industries bring to the GDP, how many jobs they create. There were more jobs in cultural and creative sectors than in the automobile sector! This is a huge potential for good and green jobs and many of those jobs are anchored in local society.

Engaging with the UN's "epistemic infrastructure" (Tichenor et al., 2022) of sustainability enabled UNESCO to address the political challenge of being an active participant in the debate and to advocate for the significance of culture in sustainable development. This infrastructure encapsulates the values of sustainability in 17 SDGs, outlined in 169 targets to be measured through 232 indicators to be achieved by 2030. It shapes the conditions of possibility for sustainable development and, more broadly, influences the conceptualization

[63] Given at the University of Geneva in September 2022.

of social issues on a global scale. Described as a "normative outlook on the world" (Sachs, 2015: 3), this framing of sustainable development creates a social imaginary of a moral order that binds together diverse cultures, embodying a tension between particularism and universalism akin to that found in Human Rights (Immler and Sakkers, 2022).

The tension between recognizing different moral understandings of sustainability and the necessity of establishing standards for global sustainable development reflects a fundamental challenge for international organizations: that of articulating a shared vision for development, establishing core priorities, holding states accountable, and managing the controversial effects of these standardizing and uniformizing endeavors. As Moore argues, on the one hand, "It seems impossible to imagine how there could be change of sufficient magnitude on so many urgent issues without setting standards and timelines for their attainment" (2015: 802). On the other, however, working within a given set of values and ideas and a reliance on standards does not "seek to challenge assumptions, but to make the system deliver" (ibid: 803). In corroborating ontological assumptions valued as universal while resulting from a particular "western-centric" perspective (Telleria, 2022), standardized representations of sustainability bear the risk of sidelining the unsettling potential of particular, situated, and alternative understandings of ways of living in society and interacting with natural environments.

4.1 Audit and the Diversity/Standardization Tension in Practice

The audit mechanisms established for evaluating the performance of States Parties in the implementation of the Convention embody this tension in practice, as they associate ICH safeguarding with SD priorities while ordering diversity into a set of indicators and benchmarks. In 2018, following the introduction of the OD on ICH and SD, an overall results framework (hereafter ORF)[64] was established. This framework was created in response to recommendations from the UNESCO Internal Oversight Service, which, in its 2013 evaluation of the Convention, requested to "enhance cooperation with sustainable development experts for integrating ICH into non-cultural legislation and policy, and for other work related to ICH and sustainable development" and to "strengthen monitoring and evaluation of the implementation of the Convention at the national level."[65]

[64] This framework was approved by the General Assembly in 2018 and covers eight thematic areas: Institutional and human capacities; Transmission and education; Inventorying and research; Policies as well as legal and administrative measures; Role of intangible cultural heritage and its safeguarding in society; Awareness raising; Engagement of communities, groups and individuals as well as other stakeholders; International engagement.

[65] IOS/EVS/PI/129 REV: 70–71.

The Internal Oversight Service emphasized in particular the need for a shift from focusing on "activities undertaken" in periodic reports to a more "result-oriented" approach that highlights "results achieved." Since measuring the results "is only possible if it is clear what results are to be achieved" the development of an overall results framework "with objectives, time-frames, quantitative and qualitative indicators, and benchmarks" was encouraged.[66] It was furthermore highlighted that a set of indicators should demonstrate how culture contributes to development. The Internal Oversight Service suggested that the monitoring process be based on the Theory of Change (Stein and Valters, 2012), valued for its ability to measure the impact of the Convention's normative work on legislative, policy-making, and policy-implementation fields.

The reflection on the ORF began with a preliminary expert meeting hosted by China in 2016, followed by an open-ended intergovernmental working group the following year. This group identified twenty-six indicators and eighty-six assessment factors to measure the effectiveness of Convention implementation. While the actual reports do not explicitly reference SDGs, guidance notes from the secretariat link each ORF indicator to specific SDG targets or assessment factors.[67] For example, the relationship between SDGs and indicator 21, measuring the "Extent to which engagement for safeguarding ICH is enhanced among stakeholders," is presented as follows:

> This indicator, by advocating wide participation in ICH safeguarding by a broad range of actors, supports SDG Target 16.7 ("ensure responsive, inclusive, participatory and representative decision-making at all levels"), as well as SDG Target 17.17, "encourage and promote effective public, public-private, and civil society partnerships." It also responds to SDG Target 11.4, which concerns protecting and safeguarding the world's cultural and natural heritage.

In turn, this ORF influenced the revision of Form ICH-10, which States Parties are required to submit every six years to detail the implementation of the Convention. While this mechanism is still in its early stages[68] and the actual effects remain unclear, the reactions of those responsible for preparing these reports underscore the "highly technical, even technocratic" nature of the process, as noted by a Swiss official overseeing periodic reporting (Vuilleumier and Hertz, 2024: 129). A former UNESCO official meanwhile observed that periodic

[66] IOS/EVS/PI/129 REV: 66–67

[67] [online] https://ich.unesco.org/en/overall-results-framework-00984#guidance-notes-by-indicators (accessed November 23, 2023).

[68] Periodic reports have been submitted only since 2021.

reporting challenged even the most organized administrations, known for complying with the requirements and principles of the Convention: "This has even gone over the heads of the good students, like the Swiss!"[69] Expanding on these observations, he argued that while the interrelation between ICH and SD can be appreciated in terms of "resonance," namely a loose interrelation allowing to associate the two concepts, the "obsession" with indicators "leads nowhere" and the "tethnicization of sustainable development" would "make it lose its potential." The "technicization of sustainable development" and its transformation into a "scientific and mathematical concept" are here considered a pretense of objectivity that is far from objective. In this perspective, the ORF and periodic reporting (PR) are seen as the "paroxysm" of an "accounting approach to the cultural field," discrediting the Convention by shifting focus from concrete intervention in ICH safeguarding to bureaucratic paperwork, described by the former UNESCO official as "red tape" ("*gratter du papier*"). In fact, this meta-dimension qualified by the aforementioned official as "policy turned into paperwork" is seen by some individuals responsible for implementing the Convention as diverting resources from more effective forms of intervention. As noted by a UNESCO facilitator familiar with periodic reporting procedures, "It's a big hassle. We put all our energy into procedures."

This elevated level of bureaucratization has produced skepticism within the organization itself, where different working cultures and sensibilities, ranging from more humanistic to more administrative, coexist. A former secretary of the Convention describes the ORF as "intricate" and periodic reporting as "cumbersome" (Smeets, 2024: 48–49). Another UNESCO official acknowledged the difficulty of the reporting requests and their perceived lack of relevance for actors on the ground: "communities are not measuring the impact of their projects; they are doing things because they consider that these things are the right thing to do." Not only is this highly technical and bureaucratic approach seen as a cause of the Convention's lack of impact but it also raises concerns about potential loss of diversity in ICH approaches due to the dominance of indicator-based language: "We come with this language of indicators, and we are losing all the other approaches." In the resigned view of a UNESCO Living Heritage unit official, this reflects the fact that, despite good intentions, "the ideology of UNESCO is very standardizing." In simpler terms, these perspectives express the concern that the auditing process is based on the assumption that SD is objective, assessable through a set of indicators, standard benchmarks, and goals presented as "universal" (Telleria, 2022).

[69] "*Même les bons élèves, comme les Suisses, ont été dépassés!*"

At the same time, however, this very technicization is regarded as a strategic move by other actors of the Convention, including some norm entrepreneurs among ICH experts or the NGOs accredited to the Convention that have proudly engaged with this process, pushing for developing qualitative rather than quantitative indicators. While acknowledging that these indicators can be "reductive," they argue that they are also a valuable "tool," which is "not narrow" but instead "leaves a lot of space" and is "very narrative, not only numbers and figures."

These actors consider PR as an opportunity to introduce complexity into the governance of the Convention, with a potentially subversive impact: "it is an enormous amount of work, an impossible bureaucratic task but the only way to make a change." In this perspective, the indicators used in PR are regarded as "a whole battery of tools that activate things." The primary function of PR, they contend, is to guide the actions of states towards SD-related policy goals, diverting attention from ICH lists: "all attention of the states usually goes to the lists. The ORF (as it is transferred in PR) is what now forces them to think in terms of sustainable development." As they argue, "the fact that the ORF and PR are closely linked to Chapter VI is a way to highlight its importance." For one representative of an active NGO accredited to the Convention, PR "gives a tool to go to the governments, and the possibility of saying: 'Hey, you can't reduce ICH to listing, it is also about local economic development, education etc.'" PR would thus allow ICH to play a role in public policies, which are seen as otherwise not interested in this heritage niche.

In other words, by "rendering technical" (Li, 2007) and measurable through indicators (Merry, 2011), audit mechanisms aim to drive change, enabling those who master the assessment techniques, such as NGOs and facilitators trained by the UNESCO secretariat and organized in national focal points, to channel policy-making toward objectives consistent with what they regard as "good" governance. In emphasizing the potential of ICH to foster SD, PR has indeed a performative power. Far from simply documenting results (Hull, 2012), reports inevitably direct actions to domains considered relevant for their assessment, facilitating the attainment of expected and verifiable results, as acknowledged by the experts involved in setting up this mechanism themselves (Blake, 2023).

In discussing the effects of PR, for instance, a senior advisor of the Finnish Heritage Agency commented that PR had lit a "lamp in her head" that allowed her to "see things much more clearly." With a wry smile, she recalled realizing, "oh, this is what the Convention is about . . ., this is what we should be doing." PR allowed her to see a "bigger connection," which she explained as an understanding of safeguarding that is "not only about keeping the old techniques in our communities but connecting to Agenda 2030 and the SDGs." An illustrative example of PR's influence on project development is the Livind project, titled "Creative and living cultural heritage as a resource for the Northern Dimension region."[70] Involving ten countries from Northern Europe, this initiative aims to "strengthen the role of intangible cultural heritage in local communities as the source of sustainable development, well-being, and livelihoods." As the project coordinator explains,

> The different skills and traditional practices encompassed in living cultural heritage contain a variety of elements that can be used to respond to challenges of today and the future, such as climate change and its side effects. Some of the solutions that are sustainable for the environment, communities and economy can be found close by, in our own inherited knowledge and skills.[71]

According to a senior advisor at the Finnish Heritage Agency, many of the pilot projects funded by Livind reflect the "educative approach" of PR. The funding scheme underscores the importance of projects that address the intersection between living heritage and sustainable development, emphasizing the role of living heritage in supporting local communities' livelihoods, stability, and well-being. The funding template specifically prompts applicants to consider how their projects strengthen living heritage as a sustainable resource for local communities and how their anticipated outcomes align with sustainable development goals. From this perspective, PR, instead of confining the concept of Sustainable Development to predefined categories or bureaucratic structures, is seen as broadening perspectives. As an NGO representative aptly put it, PR doesn't "reduce but opens up the perspectives," embodying an idealistic ambition and agency, utilizing administrative procedures to enable specific types of action and transforming bureaucracy into a vocational pursuit – an arena for utopia and moral agency (Billaud, 2015; Bortolotto, 2020b; Bortolotto et al., 2020).

If they are intended and valued as "boundary objects" carrying shared meanings and objectives while being appropriated and adapted to particular contexts (Jacobs, 2020: 272), these administrative processes seek to order and codify particular items to make them commensurable and therefore somehow able to act together. Determining which issues are considered relevant and which not, performance indicators have performative power (Billaud, 2015) and are "effectively intended as yardsticks against which governments are held to account" in evaluating their actions (Homewood, 2017: 92).

[70] https://ndpculture.org/projects/livind-creative-and-living-cultural-heritage-as-a-resource-for-the-northern-dimension-region/ (accessed November 23, 2023).

[71] https://ndpculture.org/projects/livind-creative-and-living-cultural-heritage-as-a-resource-for-the-northern-dimension-region/ (accessed November 23, 2023).

This becomes evident when local policies for safeguarding ICH don't seamlessly align with the UNESCO standards for integrating ICH and SD. A UNESCO facilitator involved in the global capacity-building program with Arabic countries views these standards as reflecting a specific perspective of Nordic countries. He recounted this approach being perceived as "very distant" by his counterparts in Arabic countries, who nonetheless find themselves drawn into this paradigm. His work with national administrations aims to develop ICH safeguarding strategies based on the same models with which the Nordic countries enthusiastically engage. New projects are specifically designed to fulfill the required criteria in periodic reports. As he acknowledged, "our framework strategy is already aligned with periodic reporting."

This necessity of conforming and aligning prompts the initiation and execution of processes intended to be measured and evaluated by these indicators. Much like Merry's observation that "an indicator may even create the phenomenon it is measuring instead of the other way around" (Merry, 2011: S84), it is clear that, in meeting the demand for measurable results, indicators guide and shape actions. Similar to the dynamics observed in the Universal Periodic Review of the Human Rights Council, as noted by Cowan, PR functions as a blend of self-coercion and voluntary engagement, along with "collective peer oversight, self-revelation, and anticipatory self-regulation" (Cowan, 2013: 118).

What is referred to in UNESCO-speak as a reporting "exercise" serves as a policy catalyst for states. As an expert involved in the design of the ORF put it, "to respond effectively to the next periodic reporting, they are implementing Chapter VI." Essentially, these administrative tools are meant to black-box the ways of interlinking ICH with SD. This social ordering serves to establish the legitimacy and validity of specific policy principles, transforming "heterogeneous elements into standardized forms which ensure manipulation, mobility, and legibility of reality" (Baya-Laffite, 2016: 238).

In creating a script for imagining the entanglement of ICH and SD, PR is perceived as bearing the risk of constraining the imaginary of sustainability, reducing it to specific objectives compatible with the standardized framework. The use of such frameworks would limit potential interventions to those aligning with predetermined goals crystallized in international principles of sustainable development rather than creatively expand the possibilities of diverse and unconventional ways of using ICH for imagining alternative ways of conceiving social welfare, the relationship with the environment or the use of natural resources. This would eventually sideline local concepts of sustainability, echoing the observations made, for example, by Katherine Homewood relative to Tanzania's Wildlife Management Areas (Homewood, 2017).

Likewise, in reflecting on his role in adapting the UNESCO standards to Arabic countries, the aforementioned facilitator commented: "It's a bit terrible, we always come back to a form of domination because the culture that people carry is not good for these boxes." Concern is thus raised about the actual "universality" of the ontological assumptions underlying global governance structures, especially those associated with the 2030 Agenda. From this perspective, periodic reporting could potentially "create an inherently ethnocentric understanding of global issues" and "perpetuate, rather than transform, the status quo" (Telleria, 2022: 621).

Meanwhile, while recognizing the practical constraints of working within an institutional framework and pragmatic compliance with its political context rather than resistance against it, norm entrepreneurs within the Convention, including civil society organizations, see this standardization as an opportunity. They view it as a means of redirecting the focus of state policies away from a pursuit of international visibility and prestige granted by listing, toward a more tangible concern for sustainability. In this sense, they leverage the highly political dimension of the ostensibly purely technical audit enterprise and consciously embrace "the art of doing politics while pretending not to" (Louis and Maertens, 2021: 2).

Conclusion

An examination of the evolution of the ICH Convention and the ways UNESCO's normative work and soft guidance integrate SD into the "authorized heritage discourse" (Smith, 2006) reveals a significant turn: ICH is increasingly portrayed as a resource for tackling the environmental, economic, and social concerns of our times. Notably, the concept of sustainability is inherently embedded in a temporal shift introduced by the ICH paradigm. Departing from a conventional model of conservation of relics of the past, this paradigm builds on the concept of safeguarding, where heritage is no longer regarded as something to be preserved. It is instead reconceptualized as a project for the future with new political and social functions. Whereas heritage was fundamentally established as an engagement with the past, the safeguarding of ICH and the idea of SD reflect a shared concern for the future and the need to change and adapt to evolving contexts and priorities.

Against this backdrop, the sustainabilization of ICH goes beyond the cultural sector. ICH is, in fact, depicted as more than a collection of cultural practices fostering social bonds and community cohesion and is increasingly recognized as a repository of knowledge and skills capable of addressing uncertainties and crises during armed conflicts, displacements, pandemics, and even apocalyptic scenarios of water shortages, hunger, forced migration, and social and political turmoil. The examples of "Avalanche Risks Management" and "Safeguarding foster care heritage in the merciful city of Geel: a community-based care model" shed light on how the ICH apparatus is used to transcend a traditional focus on preserving cultural traditions to become a versatile resource for confronting contemporary problems, including climate change and mental health issues.

Repositioned as a resource for SD, ICH has therefore been given new agency by the UNESCO policy apparatus and framed within broader and "intersectorial" governance objectives. Bureaucratic and audit tools, such as the nomination forms for inscription on the lists of the Convention and the periodic reporting system, play a crucial role in steering a paradigm shift in representations of heritage, its function, and transmission. This apparatus, structured around standard indicators and targets, gives this agency a distinct character, practically defining patterns of "good" heritage governance and thereby serving a crucial political function.

The political dimension of heritage, extensively explored in critical heritage studies over the past two decades, is primarily linked to identity claims. As a nostalgic perspective on the past, heritage is, in fact, used to make identity claims, serving to validate specific narratives while suppressing others. While the ICH framework often serves nationalist and essentialist projects on the ground, the future-oriented approach to ICH safeguarding is theoretically void of this form of nostalgia. It nevertheless remains highly political, as it advocates particular perspectives on sustainability and means of achieving the latter. The pursuit of sustainability through cultural diversity can in fact align with distinctive political endeavors, rooted in fundamentally different principles and values. For instance, the Zapatists of Chiapas articulate these endeavors in pluriversal articulations that shape "a world where many worlds fit," as asserted in the Fourth Declaration of the Lacandón Jungle, by the Ejército Zapatista de Liberación Nacional (EZLN).[72] They integrate tradition not with the modernity of the present but with projects for the future that question and challenge this modernity and its capitalist foundations (Baschet, 2018).

In contrast to the normalization of diversity, characterized by standardized and globally adopted criteria, the concept of the pluriverse encompasses diverse ways of shaping the world and living in it (Escobar, 2018). These include practices developed in the Global South, where "heterogeneous worldings come together as a political ecology of practices, negotiating their difficult being together in heterogeneity" (De la Cadena and Blaser, 2018: 4). Here,

[72] https://enlacezapatista.ezln.org.mx/1996/01/01/cuarta-declaracion-de-la-selva-lacandona/ (Accessed December 30, 2023).

conceptions of "good" and sustainable life involve individuals reconnecting with being a modest component of the natural world, moving away from limited anthropocentric notions of progress driven by economic expansion. Profoundly shaped by decolonizing ambitions, the ideals shaping the movements promoting indigenous concepts and worldviews are echoed by other perspectives, such as degrowth, commons, or ecofeminism advocated in the Western world (Larsen et al., 2022: 24). However, as Kothari et al. argue, the kind of political engagement underlying these different movements calling for radical transformations of our society "cannot be reduced to an overarching policy for administration either by the UN or some other global governance regime" (Kothari et al., 2019: xxviii) or to "the universalizing ideology of sustainable development" (Kothari et al., 2019: xxviii). From this standpoint, UN SD narratives do not entail a commitment to fundamental change addressing structural problems but instead allow a conservative reproduction of the existing, growth-oriented world order, simply extending capitalism into a green variant of itself (Brightman and Lewis, 2017).

Emerging within the dominant political-economic context that shapes contemporary societies, the UNESCO approach to "good" governance of ICH resonates with the values of this political context, often blamed for reflecting essentially Northern concerns and outlooks on cultural transmission or interaction with the natural world and thereby black-boxing their sustainability potential (Herzfeld, 2010; De Cesari, 2012; Meskell, 2013; Coombe and Weiss, 2015). Despite the fact that individuals promoting key principles of good ICH governance often engage with it as adamant opponents of political and economic forces frequently qualified with the shorthand expression of neoliberalism, the UNESCO ICH apparatus operates within and as a product of this system, rather than as a form of resistance against it (Scher, 2010; De Cesari et al., 2020). As a resource for new forms of capital accumulation (Boltanski and Esquerre, 2020), heritage proves here to be connected to capitalism in a dual relation of dependence and resistance, as has been observed in its local uses (Clifford, 2013: 238). Numerous readings of the UNESCO heritage apparatus through a Foucauldian lens have highlighted that what is deemed "good" governance of ICH mirrors, in fact, essential characteristics of neoliberal logics, from "entrepreneurial self-government" (Dardot and Laval, 2013) to the "neoliberal language of stakeholding" (Strathern, 2012: 116), encompassing concepts such as empowerment or community participation (Coombe, 2011). Hafstein and Skrydstrupn propose that ICH, representing a "technology of reformation" based on bottom-up approaches, community participation, and voluntarism, contributes to cultivating proactive, responsible subjects and is "part of a larger turn to governmentality in the politics of the past decades" (Hafstein and Skrydstrup, 2017: 48).[73]

As a specialized agency of the UN, UNESCO operates within the established system rather than opposing it as an independent radical activist, such as the Zapatist combatants. UNESCO does not advocate *resistance* against the political and economic forces shaping society but proposes a *transition* deeply entwined with them.[74] Against this backdrop, the motto underpinning the sustainabilization of ICH is "resilience" characterized by Hornborg as the "rallying-cry of the early twenty-first century" as opposed to "revolution," seen as the call of the early twentieth century (Hornborg, 2009: 252). Embedded in the semantic field of sustainable development, resilience is championed in the ICH discourse as a cornerstone of sustainability, capable of addressing both chronic and disruptive crises. In this, it is not only the original bearers of particular social and cultural practices but humanity at large, drawing on and adapting those practices, that can "bounce back" and "build back" using knowledge and skills transmitted across generations.

In emphasizing accommodation and celebrating the human skills that make the latter possible, resilience has, however, came under scrutiny as a "compromised concept" (Noyes, 2006), embodying, like SD, a "win-win language" (Larsen et al., 2022: 21) aimed at de-politicizing crisis, mitigating radical reactions, and paving the way for "neoliberal adaptation" (Hirsch, 2020: 12). As Neocleous puts it, "resilience wants acquiescence, not resistance. Not a passive acquiescence, for sure, in fact quite the opposite. But it does demand that we use our actions to accommodate ourselves to capital and the state, and the secure future of both, rather than to resist them" (Neocleous, 2013: 7).

Shaped by contemporary values like resilience, heritage continues to be a highly controversial and political field as well as a constructed and evolving concept, reflecting changing historical, cultural, and political contexts. The social and political applications of this broadened heritage field on the part of

[73] Scher goes as far as to contend that the 2003 Convention can be interpreted as a symbol of UNESCO's neoliberal shift, where the return of the USA precisely in 2003 – after withdrawing in 1984 from what they regarded as an agent of socialism, hostile to free market – was not a coincidence. He argues this reversal provides evidence of the fact that "UNESCO had, in the eyes of the United States, moved to a position with regard to neoliberalism that suited the interests of the country" (2010: 199).

[74] According to historians of energy, the concept of transition is misleading and climate change requires a civilization change rather than a technology change (Fressoz, 2024: 15). This vocabulary is seen by the more radical critiques of the SD concept as a way of referring to projects that avoid fundamental social, ecological, or energetic transformation in addressing cultural, social, and ecological concerns and regarded instead as complying with priorities of economic growth and business-as-usual resource extraction (*Vocabulaire critique & spéculatif des transitions*), [online] https://vocabulairedestransitions.fr/ (Accessed September 25, 2023).

future generations will likely differ significantly from what we have witnessed thus far, as noted by Holtorf (2022). Despite the structural limitations mentioned earlier, this expansion is seen by many "heritage believers" (Brumann, 2014) as opening up new and potentially refreshing perspectives on heritage. For several of my interlocutors, approaching heritage as a forward-looking project to build upon, rather than an inheritance of the past to identify with in order to claim ancestry, is enough to serve as a source of hope.

References

Angé, O. and Berliner, D. (2020) "Introduction," in *Ecological Nostalgias Memory, Affect and Creativity in Times of Ecological Upheaval*. New York: Berghahn Books, pp. 1–16.

Appréderisse, C. (2019) *Patrimoine culturel immatériel et développement durable. L'incidence juridique de la notion de développement durable dans la Convention pour la sauvegarde du patrimoine culturel immatériel*. Québec: Teseo Press.

Arizpe, L. (2004) "The Intellectual History of Culture and Development Institutions," in Rao, V. and Walton, M. (eds) *Culture and Public Action*. Stanford: Stanford University Press, pp. 163–184.

Aykan, B. (2015) "'Patenting' Karagöz: UNESCO, Nationalism and Multinational Intangible Heritage," *International Journal of Heritage Studies*. Routledge, 21(10), pp. 949–961. https://doi.org/10.1080/13527258.2015.1041413.

Aykan, B. (2016) "The Politics of Intangible Heritage and Food Fights in Western Asia," *International Journal of Heritage Studies ISSN*, 22(10), pp. 799–810. https://doi.org/10.1080/13527258.2016.1218910.

Aykut, S. C. and Maertens, L. (2021) "The Climatization of Global Politics: Introduction to the Special Issue," *International Politics*. Palgrave Macmillan, 58(4), pp. 501–518. https://doi.org/10.1057/s41311-021-00325-0.

Aykut, S. C., Foyer, J. and Morena, E. (eds) (2017) *Globalising the Climate: COP21 and the Climatisation of Global Debates*. London and New York: Routledge.

Bargheer, S. (2016) "Conserving the Future UNESCO Biosphere Reserves as Laboratories for Sustainable Development," in Vidal, F. and Dias, N. (eds) *Endangerment, Biodiversity and Culture, Endangerment, Biodiversity and Culture*. London and New York: Routledge, pp. 115–133.

Baschet, J. (2018) *Défaire la tyrannie du présent: Témporalités émergentes et futurs inédits*. Paris: La Découverte.

Baya-Laffite, N. (2016) "Black-Boxing Sustainable Development: Environmental Impact Assessment on the River Uruguay," in Voß, J. and Freeman, R. (eds) *Knowing Governance. Palgrave Studies in Science, Knowledge and Policy*. London: Palgrave Macmillan, pp. 237–255. https://doi.org/10.1057/9781137514509.

Berliner, D. (2012) "Multiple Nostalgias: The Fabric of Heritage in Luang Prabang (Lao PDR)," *Journal of the Royal Anthropological Institute*, 18(4), pp. 769–786. https://doi.org/10.1111/j.1467-9655.2012.01791.x.

Berliner, D. (2018) *Perdre sa culture*. Bruxelles: Zones sensibles.

Betts, P. (2015) "The Warden of World Heritage: UNESCO and the Rescue of the Nubian Monuments," *Past & Present*, 226(suppl_10), pp. 100–125. https://doi.org/10.1093/pastj/gtu017.

Bierschenk, T. (2014) "From the Anthropology of Development to the Anthropology of Global Social Engineering," *Zeitschrift für Ethnologie*, 139(1), pp. 73–97.

Billaud, J. (2015) "Keepers of the Truth: Producing 'Transparent' Documents for the Universal Periodic Review," in H. Charlesworth and E. Larking (ed.) *Human Rights and the Universal Periodic Review: Rituals and Ritualism*. Cambridge: Cambridge University Press, pp. 63–84.

Billaud, J. and Cowan, J. K. (2020) "The Bureaucratisation of Utopia: Ethics, Affects and Subjectivities in International Governance Processes," *Social Anthropology*, 28(1), pp. 6–16. https://doi.org/10.1111/1469-8676.12750.

Blake, J. (2020) "The Preamble," in Blake, J. and Lixinski, L. (eds) *The 2003 UNESCO Intangible Heritage Convention: A Commentary*. Oxford: Oxford University Press, pp. 19–35.

Blake, J. (2023) *Safeguarding Intangible Cultural Heritage: A Practical Interpretation of the 2003 UNESCO Convention*. Cheltenham: Edward Elgar.

Blake, J. (2024) "Sustainable Development and Human Rights in Safeguarding ICH: Positive Goals or an Internal Contradiction?" in Bortolotto, C. and Skounti, A. (eds) *Intangible Cultural Heritage and Sustainable Development: Inside a UNESCO Convention*. London and New York: Routledge, pp. 19–35.

Boccardi, G. and Scott, L. (2018) "A View from the Inside an Account of the Process Leading to the Adoption of the Policy for the Integration of a Sustainable Development Perspective within the World Heritage Convention," in Larsen, P. B. and Logan, W. (eds) *World Heritage and Sustainable Development: New Directions in World Heritage Management*. London: Routledge, pp. 21–36.

Boltanski, L. and Esquerre, A. (2020) *Enrichment: A Critique of Commodities*. Cambridge: Polity Press.

Bortolotto, C. (2011) "Le trouble du patrimoine culturel immatériel," in Bortolotto, C. (ed.) *Le patrimoine culturel immatériel: enjeux d'une nouvelle catégorie*. Paris: Éditions de la Maison des sciences de l'homme, pp. 21–43. http://terrain.revues.org/14447.

Bortolotto, C. (2013) "L'Unesco comme arène de traduction: La fabrique globale du patrimoine immatériel," *Gradhiva*. Musée du quai Branly, (18), pp. 50–73. https://doi.org/10.4000/gradhiva.2708.

Bortolotto, C. (2014) "Le transfert d'un standard international: le patrimoine culturel immatériel vu par la France," in Bondaz, J., Graezer Bideau, F.,

Isnart, C., and Leblon, A. (eds) *Vocabulaires locaux du « patrimoine ». Traductions, négociations et transformations*. Berlin: Lit Verlag, pp. 107–122.

Bortolotto, C. (2015) "UNESCO and Heritage Self-Determination: Negotiating Meaning in the Intergovernmental Committee for the Safeguarding of the ICH," in Adell, N., Bendix, R. F., Bortolotto, C., and Tauschek, M. (eds) *Between Imagined Communities and Communities of Practice: Participation, Territoritory and the Making of Heritage*. Göttingen: Göttingen University Press, pp. 249–272.

Bortolotto, C. (2017a) "Collaborative Dilemmas in the Age of Uncertainty." https://allegralaboratory.net/collaborative-dilemmas-in-the-age-of-uncertainty/.

Bortolotto, C. (2017b) "Como comerse un patrimonio: construir bienes inmateriales agroalimentarios entre directivas técnicas y empresariado patrimonial," *Revista Andaluza de Antropología*, 12, pp. 144–166.

Bortolotto, C. (2020a) "Le patrimoine immatériel et le tabou de l'authenticité: de la pérennisation à la durabilité," in Csergo, J., Hottin, C., and Schmit, P. (eds) *Le patrimoine culturel immatériel au seuil des sciences sociales*. Paris: Éditions de la Maison des sciences de l'homme, pp. 218–235 [online]. https://doi.org/10.4000/books.editionsmsh.16377.

Bortolotto, C. (2020b) "Let's Get Together: The Making of Shared Heritage between Bureaucratization of Utopia and Utopianization of Bureaucracy," *L'Espace géographique*, 49(4), pp. 319–336.

Bortolotto, C. (2021) "Commercialization without Over-commercialization: Normative Conundrums across Heritage Rationalities', *International Journal of Heritage Studies*. Routledge, 27(9), pp. 857–868. https://doi.org/10.1080/13527258.2020.1858441.

Bortolotto, C. (2024) "The Embarrassment of Heritage Alienability," *Current Anthropology*. 65(1), pp. 100–122. https://doi.org/10.1086/728686.

Bortolotto, C. and Ubertazzi, B. (2018) "Editorial: Foodways as Intangible Cultural Heritage," *International Journal of Cultural Property*, 25(4), pp. 409–418. https://doi.org/10.1017/S0940739119000055.

Bortolotto, C. and Skounti, A. (2024) "The Rise of Sustainable Development in the Convention for the Safeguarding of the Intangible Cultural Heritage," in Bortolotto, C. and Skounti, A. (eds) *Intangible Cultural heritage and Sustainable Development: Inside a UNESCO Convention*. London and New York: Routledge, pp. 1–16.

Bortolotto, C., Demgenski, P., Karampampas, P., and Toji, S. (2020) "Proving Participation: Vocational Bureaucrats and Bureaucratic Creativity in the Implementation of the UNESCO Convention for the Safeguarding of the

Intangible Cultural Heritage," *Social Anthropology*, 28(1), pp. 66–82. https://doi.org/10.1111/1469-8676.12741.

Breithoff, E. and Harrison, R. (2020) "Banking Time: Trading in Futures," in Harrison, R., DeSilvey, C., Holtorf, C., et al. (eds) *Heritage Futures: Comparative Approaches to Natural and Cultural Heritage Practices*. London: UCL Press, pp. 101–120.

Brightman, M. and Lewis, J. (2017) "Introduction: The Anthropology of Sustainability: Beyond Development and Progress," in Brightman, M. and Lewis, J. (eds) *The Anthropology of Sustainability: Beyond Development and Progress*. New York: Palgrave Macmillan, pp. 1–34. https://doi.org/10.1057/978-1-137-56636-2.

Brumann, C. (2013) "Comment le patrimoine mondial de l'Unesco devient immatériel," *Gradhiva*, 18, pp. 22–49.

Brumann, C. (2014) "Heritage Agnosticism: A Third Path for the Study of Cultural Heritage," *Social Anthropology*, 22(2), pp. 173–188. https://doi.org/10.1111/1469-8676.12068.

Brumann, C. (2021) *The Best We Share: Nation, Culture and World-Making in the UNESCO World Heritage Arena*. New York: Berghahn.

Carneiro da Cunha, M. (2017) "Traditional People, Collectors of Diversity," in Brightman, M. and Lewis, J. (eds) *The Anthropology of Sustainability: Beyond Development and Progress*. New York: Palgrave Macmillan, pp. 257–272.

Ceribašić, N. (2019) "On Engaging up and Expertisein Ethnomusicology: The Example of Expert Services in the Programme for Safeguarding Intangible Cultural Heritage," in Hemetek, U., Kölbl, M., and Sağlam, H. (eds) *Ethnomusicology Matters: Influencing Social and Political Realities*. Wien: Bohlau Verlag, pp. 233–256. https://doi.org/10.7767/9783205232872.233.

de Certeau, M., Julia, D., and Revel, J. (1970) "La beauté du mort: le concept de culture populaire," *Politique aujourd'hui*, 12, pp. 3–23.

De Cesari, C. (2012) "Thinking through Heritage Regimes," in Bendix, R., Eggert, A., and Peselmann, A. (eds) *Heritage Regimes and the State*. Göttingen: Göttingen University Press, pp. 399–413.

De Cesari, C., Bshara, K., Clarke, J., et al. (2020) "Heritage beyond the Nation-State?: Nongovernmental Organizations, Changing Cultural Policies, and the Discourse of Heritage as Development," *Current Anthropology*, 61(1), pp. 30–56. http://10.0.4.62/707208.

Chave, I. (2021) "Patrimoine culturel immatériel, nature et environnement: entre bilans et promesses," *Les Cahiers du CFPCI*, 8, pp. 9–15.

Chong, J. W. (2012) "'Mine, Yours or Ours?': The Indonesia-Malaysia Disputes over Shared Cultural Heritage," *Sojourn*, 27(1), pp. 1–53. https://doi.org/10.1355/sj27-1a.

Cianconi, P., Hanife, B., Grillo, F., et al. (2023) "Eco-emotions and Psychoterratic Syndromes: Reshaping Mental Health Assessment under Climate Change," *The Yale Journal of Biology and Medicine*, 96(2), pp. 211–226. https://doi.org/10.59249/earx2427.

Clayton, S., Manning, C. M., Krygsman, K., Speiser, M. (2017) *Mental Health and Our Changing Climate: Impacts, Implications, and Guidance*. Washington, DC: American Psychological Association, ecoAmerica. http://doi.apa.org/get-pe-doi.cfm?doi=10.1037/e503122017-001.

Clifford, J. (2004) "Traditional Futures," in Hillips, M. S. and Schochet, G. (eds) *Questions of Tradition*. Toronto: University of Toronto Press, pp. 152–168. https://doi.org/10.3138/9781442678958-007.

Clifford, J. (2013) *Returns: Becoming Indigenous in the Twenty-First Century*. Edited by H. U. Press. Cambridge, MA: Harvard University.

Comaroff, J. L. and Comaroff, J. (2009) *Ethnicity, Inc*. Chicago: University of Chicago Press.

Coombe, R. J. (2011) "Cultural Agencies: 'Constructing' Community Subjects and their Rights," in Biagioli, J., Jaszi, P., and Woodmansee, M. (eds) *Making and Unmaking Intellectual Property*. Chicago: University of Chicago Press, pp. 79–98. https://doi.org/10.4324/9780429058981-9.

Coombe, R. J. and Weiss, L. M. (2015) "Neoliberalism, Heritage Regimes, and Cultural Rights," in Meskell, L. (ed) *Global Heritage: A Reader*. Hoboken, NJ: Wiley Blackwel, pp. 43–69.

Cowan, J. (2013) "Before Audit Culture: A Genealogy of International Oversight of Rights," in Müller, B. (ed.) *The Gloss of Harmony The Politics of Policy-Making in Multilateral Organisations*. London: Pluto Press, pp. 103–133.

Curtis, T. (2002) *Talking about Place: Identities, Histories and Powers among the Na'hai Speakers of Malakula (Vanuatu)*. Camberra: The Australian National University.

Curtis, T. (2017) "Intangible Cultural Heritage at the Heart of Sustainable Development," in Schreiber, H. (ed.) *Intangible Cultural Heritage: Safeguarding Experiences in Central and Eastern European Countries and China: The 10th Anniversary of the Entry into Force of the 2003 Convention through the Prism of Sustainable Development*. Warsaw: National Heritage Board of Poland, pp. 12–15.

Dardot, P. and Laval, C. (2013) *The New Way of the World: On Neo-liberal Society*. London and New York: Verso Books.

Deacon, H. and Smeets, R. (2013) "Authenticity, Value and Community Involvement in Heritage Management under the World Heritage and Intangible Heritage Conventions," *Heritage and Society*, 6(2), pp. 1–15.

DeSilvey, C. and Harrison, R. (2019) "Anticipating Loss: Rethinking Endangerment in Heritage Futures," *International Journal of Heritage Studies*. Routledge, 26 (1), pp. 1–7. https://doi.org/10.1080/13527258.2019.1644530.

Duvelle, C., Lixinski, L., and Schreiber, H. (2017) "We Need to Make Synergies between the Conventions. This is the Next Step for UNESCO . . .," *Santander Art and Culture Law Review*, 3 (2), pp. 21–32. https://doi.org/10.4467/2450050XSNR.17.019.8420.

Escobar, A. (2018) *Designs for the Pluriverse: Radical Interdependence, Autonomy, and the Making of Worlds*. Durham and London: Duke University Press.

Fabre, D. (2013) "Le patrimoine porté par l'émotion," in Fabre, D. (ed.) *Émotions patrimoniales*. Paris: Éditions de la Maison des sciences de l'homme, pp. 13–98.

Finnemore, M. and Sikkink, K. (1998) "International Norm Dynamics and Political Change," *International Organization*, 52(4), pp. 887–917. https://doi.org/10.1017/S0020818300028460.

Fisher, W. F. (1997) "DOING GOOD ? The Politics and Antipolitics of NGO Practices," *Annual Review of Anthropology*, 26, pp. 439–64.

Foster, M. D. (2011) "The UNESCO Effect: Confidence, Defamiliarization, and a New Element in the Discourse on a Japanese Island," *Journal of Folklore Research*, 48(1), pp. 63–107. https://doi.org/10.2979/jfolkrese.48.1.63.

Foucault, M. (1975) *Surveiller et punir: Naissance de la prison*. Paris: Gallimard.

Foyer, J. and Dumoulin Kervran, D. (2017) "Objectifying Traditional Knowledge, Re-enchanting the Struggle against Climate Change," in Aykut, S. C., Foyer, J., and Morena, E. (eds) *Globalising the Climate: COP21 and the Climatisation of Global Debates*. London: Routledge, pp. 153–172.

Fressoz, J.-B. (2024) *Sans transition: Une nouvelle histoire de l'energie*. Seuil, *Andrew's Disease of the Skin Clinical Dermatology*. Paris: Seuil.

Graham, M. (2002) "Emotional Bureaucracies: Emotions, Civil Servants, and Immigrants in the Swedish Welfare State," *Ethos*, 30(3), pp. 199–226.

Hafstein, V. T. (2009) "Intangible Heritage as a List: From Masterpieces to Representation," in Smith, L. and Akagawa, N. (eds) *Intangible Heritage*. London: Routledge, pp. 93–111.

Hafstein, V. T. and Skrydstrup, M. (2017) "Heritage Vs. Property: Contrasting Regimes and Rationalities in the Patrimonial Field," in Anderson, J. and

Geismar, H. (eds) *Routledge Companion to Cultural Property*. Oxford and New York: Routledge, pp. 38–53.

Harrison, R. (2020) "Heritage as Future-making Practices," in Harrison, R., DeSilvey, C., Holtorf, C., et al. (eds) *Heritage Futures: Comparative Approaches to Natural and Cultural Heritage Practices*. London: UCL Press, pp. 20–50.

Harrison, R., DeSilvey, C., Holtorf, C., et al. (2020) *Heritage Futures: Comparative Approaches to Natural and Cultural Heritage Practices*. London: UCL Press. https://doi.org/10.14324/111.9781787356009.

Hartog, F. (2003) *Régimes d'historicité: Présentisme et expérience du temps*. Paris: Le Seuil.

Harvey, D. C. (2001) "Heritage Pasts and Heritage Presents: Temporality, Meaning and the Scope of Heritage Studies," *International Journal of Heritage Studies*, 7(4), pp. 319–338. https://doi.org/10.1080/13581650120105534.

Herzfeld, M. (2005) *Cultural Intimacy: Social Poetics in the Nation-State*. 2nd ed. London: Routledge.

Herzfeld, M. (2010) "Engagement, Gentrification, and the Neoliberal Hijacking of History," *Current Anthropology*, 52(51), pp. S259–S267. https://doi.org/10.1086/653420.

Hirsch, E. (2020) "Sustainable Development," in M. Aldenderfer, M. (ed.), *Oxford Research Encyclopedia of Anthropology*. Oxford University Press.

Holtorf, C. (2020) "Conservation and Heritage as Creative Processes of Future-making," *International Journal of Cultural Property*, 27(2), pp. 277–290. https://doi.org/10.1017/S0940739120000107.

Holtorf, C. (2022) "Teaching Futures Literacy for the Heritage Sector," in Fouseki, K. et al. (eds) *Routledge Handbook of Sustainable Heritage*. London and New York: Routledge, pp. 527–542. https://doi.org/10.4324/9781003038955-42.

Holtorf, C. and Högberg, A. (2021) "Cultural Heritage as a Futuristic Field," in Holtorf, C. and Högberg, A. (eds) *Cultural Heritage and the Future brings*. London and New York: Routtledge, pp. 1–28. https://doi.org/10.18866/biaa2015.048.

Homewood, K. M. (2017) "'They Call It Shangri-La': Sustainable Conservation, or African Enclosures?" in Brightman, M. and Lewis, J. (eds) *The Anthropology of Sustainability: Beyond Development and Progress*. New York: Palgrave Macmillan, pp. 91–109.

Hornborg, A. (2009) "Zero-Sum World: Challenges in Conceptualizing Environmental Load Displacement and Ecologically Unequal Exchange in the World-System," *International Journal of Comparative Sociology*, 50(3–4), pp. 237–262. https://doi.org/10.1177/0020715209105141.

Hull, M. S. (2012) "Documents and Bureaucracy," *Annual Review of Anthropology*, 41(1), pp. 251–267. https://doi.org/10.1146/annurev.anthro.012809.104953.

ICOMOS (1964) The Venice Charter: International Charter for the Conservation and Restoration of Monuments and Sites [online], https://www.icomos.org/en/participer/179-articles-en-francais/ressources/charters-and-standards/157-the-venice-charter (accessed September 24, 2024).

Immler, N. L. and Sakkers, H. (2022) "The UN-Sustainable Development Goals Going Local: Learning from Localising Human Rights," *International Journal of Human Rights*, 26(2), pp. 262–284. https://doi.org/10.1080/13642987.2021.1913411.

Isnart, C. and Testa, A. (2024) "Reconfigurando a noção de tradição na Europa: uma introdução ao tema," *Revista Antropolítica*, 56(1), pp. 1–25.

Jacobs, M. (2020) "Words Matter. . .The Arsenal and the Repertoire: UNESCO, ICOM and European Frameworks," *Wolkskunde*, 3, pp. 267–286. https://doi.org/10.1016/j.chest.2023.01.021.

Jacobs, M. (2024) "How and Why the SDGs Entered the Paradigm of Safeguarding Intangible Heritage: The 'Sixth Chapter'," in Bortolotto, C. and Skounti, A. (eds) *Intangible Cultural Heritage and Sustainable Development: Inside a UNESCO Convention*. London and New York: Routledge, pp. 55–70.

Jacobs, M. and Neyrinck, J. (2020) "Transforming, Not Saving: Intangible Cultural Heritage, Museums and/or the World," *Volkskunde*, 3, pp. 481–502.

Kirshenblatt-gimblett, B. (2024) "Anticipatory Heritage," *Journal of American Folklore*, 137(543), pp. 85–93.

Kirshenblatt-Gimblett, B. (1998) *Destination Culture: Tourism, Museums, and Heritage*. Berkeley: University of California Press.

Kono, T. (2007) "UNESCO and Intangible Cultural Heritage from the Viewpoint of Sustainable Development," in Yusuf, A. (ed.) *Standard-Setting in UNESCO Volume 1: Normative Action in Education, Science and Culture*. Leiden: Martinus Nijhoff, pp. 237–265.

Kothari, A., Salleh, A., Escobar, A., et al. (2019) "Introduction: Finding Pluriversal Paths," in *Pluriverse: A Post-Development Dictionary*. Tulika Books, pp. xxi–xl.

De la Cadena, M. and Blaser, M. (2018) "Pluriverse: Proposals for a World of Many Worlds," in De la Cadena, M. and Blaser, M. (eds) *A World of Many Worlds*. Durham and London: Duke University Press.

Labadi, S. (2022) *Rethinking Heritage for Sustainable Development*. London: UCL Press.

Labadi, S. and Gould, P. (2015) "Sustainable Development: Heritage, Community, Economics," in Meskell, L. (ed.) *Global Heritage: A Reader*. Oxford: Wiley-Blackwell, pp. 196–216.

Larsen, P. B. (2013) "The Politics of Technicality: Guidance Culture in Environmental Governance," in Müller, B. (ed.) *The Gloss of Harmony: The Politics of Policy-Making in Multilateral Organisations*. London: Pluto Press, pp. 75–100.

Larsen, P., Haller, T., and Kothari, A. (2022) "Sanctioning Disciplined Grabs (SDGs): From SDGs as Green Anti-Politics Machine to Radical Alternatives?" *Geoforum*. Elsevier Ltd, 131(March), pp. 20–26. https://doi.org/10.1016/j.geoforum.2022.02.007.

Larsen, P., Bacalzo, D., Naef, P., et al. (2022) "Repositioning Engaged Anthropology: Critical Reflexivity and Overcoming Dichotomies," *TSANTSA – Journal of the Swiss Anthropological Association*, 27, pp. 4–15. https://doi.org/10.36950/tsantsa.2022.27.7994.

Laszczkowski, M. and Reeves, M. (2015) "Introduction: Affective States–Entanglements, Suspensions, Suspicions," *Social Analysis*, 59(4), pp. 1–14. https://doi.org/10.3167/sa.2015.590401.

Latour, B. (2017) *Facing Gaia: Eight Lectures on the New Climatic Regime*. Cambridge: Polity Press.

Lenclud, G. (1987) "La tradition n'est plus ce qu'elle était . . . ," *Terrain*, 9, pp. 110–123.

Li, T. M. (2007) *The Will to Improve: Governmentality, Development, and the Practice of Politics*. Durham: Duke University Press.

Lixinski, L. (2014) "Sustainable Development in International Heritage Law: Embracing a Backwards Look for the Sake of Forwardness?" *Australian Year Book of International Law*, 32(April), pp. 65–86. https://doi.org/10.22145/aybil.32.4.

Louis, M. and Maertens, L. (2021) *Why International Organizations Hate Politics: Depoliticizing the World*. London and New York: Routledge.

Lowenthal, D. (1998) *The Heritage Crusade and the Spoils of History*. Cambridge: Cambridge University Press.

Macdonald, S. (2013) *Memorylands: Heritage and Identity in Europe Today*. London and New York: Routledge.

Martino, M. (2014) "La gestion di risque d'avalanches? Drôle de tradition vivante!" *Le Matin*, 13(octobre) p. 2.

Masco, J. (2017) "The Crisis in Crisis," *Current Anthropology*, 58(February), pp. S65–S76. https://doi.org/10.1086/688695.

Mathur, N. (2017) "Bureaucracy," in Stein, F., Lazar, M., Candea, H., et al. (eds) *The Cambridge Encyclopedia of Anthropology*. www.anthroencyclopedia.com/entry/bureaucracy#h2ref-3.

Mayor, F. (1988) "The World Decade for Cultural Development," *The UNESCO Courier: A Window Open on the World*, 41(11), pp. 4–6.

Merry, S. E. (2011) "Measuring the World Indicators, Human Rights, and Global Governance," *Current Anthropology*, 52(SUPPL. 3), pp. 83–95. https://doi.org/10.1086/657241.

Meskell, L. (2012) *The Nature of Heritage: The New South Africa*. Oxford: Wiley-Blackwell.

Meskell, L. (2013) "UNESCO and the Fate of the World Heritage Indigenous Peoples Council of Experts (WHIPCOE)," *International Journal of Cultural Property*, 20(2), pp. 155–174. https://doi.org/10.1017/S0940739113000039.

Meskell, L. (2018) *A Future in Ruins: UNESCO, World Heritage, and the Dream of Peace*. London: Oxford University Press.

Monsutti, A. and Pétric, B.-M. (2009) "New Political Arenas: International and Non-Governmental Organizations, Foundations, Think Tanks," *Tsantsa*, 14, pp. 6–16.

Moore, H. L. (2015) "Global Prosperity and Sustainable Development Goals," *Journal of International Development*, 27(6), pp. 801–815. wileyonlinelibrary.com.

Müller, B. (2013) *The Gloss of Harmony: The Politics of Policy Making in Multilateral Organisations*. Edited by B. Müller. London: Pluto Press.

Navaro-Yashin, Y. (2006) "Affect in the Civil Service: A Study of a Modern State-System," *Postcolonial Studies: Culture, Politics, Economy*, 9(3), pp. 281–294. https://doi.org/10.1080/13688790600824997.

Neocleous, M. (2013) "Resisting Resilience," *Radical Philosophy*, 178, pp. 2–7.

Nora, P. (1997) "Entre Mémoire et Histoire. La problématique des lieux," in Nora, P. (ed.) *Les lieux de mémoire, vol. 1*. Paris: Gallimard, pp. 23–43.

Noyes, D. (2006) "The Judgment of Solomon: Global Protections for Tradition and the Problem of Community Ownership," *Cultural Analysis*, 5, pp. 27–56. https://doi.org/10.2979/humbletheory.0.0.14.

Olivier de Sardan, J.-P. (1995) *Anthropologie de developpement: essai en socioanthropologie du changement social*. Paris: Karthala. https://doi.org/10.2307/1161283.

Phillips, M. (2004) "Introduction," in Phillips, M. and Schochet, G. (eds) *Questions of Tradition*. Toronto: University of Toronto Press, pp. 3–29.

Roigé Ventura, X. and Ossul Canals, A. (eds) (2021) *Patrimonios confinados: Retos del patrimonio inmaterial ante el COVID-19*. Barcelona: Universitat de Barcelona.

Sachs, J. D. (2015) *The Age of Sustaiable Developemet*. New York: Columbia University Press. https://doi.org/10.1007/s00382.

Sapignoli, M. (2017) "A Kaleidoscopic Institutional Form: Expertise and Transformation in the UN Permanent Forum on Indigenous Issues," in Sapignoli, M. and Niezen, R. (eds) *Palaces of Hope: The Anthropology of Global Organization*. Cambridge: Cambridge University Press, pp. 78–105.

Scher, P. W. (2010) "UNESCO Conventions and Culture as a Resource," *Journal of Folklore Research: An International Journal of Folklore and Ethnomusicology*, 47(1–2), pp. 197–202. https://doi.org/10.2979/JFR.2010.47.1-2.197.

Smeets, R. (2024) "The Reorientation of a Convention: UNESCO, Intangible Heritage, and Sustainable Development," in Bortolotto, C. and Skounti, A. (eds) *Intangible Cultural Heritage and Sustainable Development: Inside a UNESCO Convention*. London: Routledge, pp. 36–54.

Smith, L. (2006) *Uses of Heritage*. London and New York: Routledge.

Sodikoff, G. M. (ed.) (2012) *The Anthropology of Extinction: Essays on Culture and Species Death*. Bloomington: Indiana University Press.

Stein, D. and Valters, C. (2012) *Understanding Theory of Change in International Development*. London: London School of Economics and Political Science.

Stengers, I. (2009) *Au temps des catastrophes. Résister à la barbarie qui vient*. Paris: La Découverte.

Stoler, A. L. (2007) "Affective States," in Nugent, D. and Vincent, J. (eds) *A Companion to the Anthropology of Politics*. Oxford: Blackwell, pp. 4–20. https://doi.org/10.1002/9780470693681.ch1.

Strathern, M. (2000) *Audit Cultures: Anthropological Studies in Accountability, Ethics and the Academy*. London and NewYork: Routledge.

Strathern, M. (2012) "Currencies of Collaboration," in Konrad, M. (ed.) *Collaborators Collaborating: Counterparts in Anthropological Knowledge and International Research Relations*. New York and Oxford: Berghahn Books, pp. 109–125.

Telleria, J. (2022) "Diversity vs the 2030 Agenda: A Deconstructive Reading of the United Nations Agenda for Sustainable Development," *Critical Social Policy*, 42(4), pp. 607–625. https://doi.org/10.1177/02610183211065699.

The Athens Charter for the Restoration of Historic Monuments (1931) [online], https://www.icomos.org/en/167-the-athens-charter-for-the-restoration-of-historic-monuments (accessed September 24, 2024).

Tichenor, M., Merry, S. E., Grek, S. Bandola-Gill, J. (2022) "Global Public Policy in a Quantified World: Sustainable Development Goals as Epistemic Infrastructures," *Policy and Society*, 41(4), pp. 431–444. https://doi.org/10.1093/polsoc/puac015.

Tornatore, J. (2014) "Words for Expressing What We Care About: The Continuity and the Exteriority of the Heritage Experience," in Bondaz, J., Graezer Bideau, F., Isnart, C., Leblon, A. (eds) *Les Vocabulaires locaux du « patrimoine ». Traductions, négociations et transformations*. Zürich and London: Lit Verlag, pp. 31–53.

Tornatore, J.-L. (2017) "Patrimoine vivant et contributions citoyennes: Penser le patrimoine «devant» l'Anthropocène," *In Situ*, (33), pp. 1–26. https://doi.org/10.4000/insitu.15606.

Trowbridge, J., Tan, J. Y., Hussain, S., et al. (2022) "Examining Intersectoral Action as an Approach to Implementing Multistakeholder Collaborations to Achieve the Sustainable Development Goals," *International Journal of Public Health*, 67(May), pp. 1–8. https://doi.org/10.3389/ijph.2022.1604351.

Tsing, A. L. (2015) *The Mushroom at the End of the World: On the Possibility of Life in Capitalist Ruins*. Princeton: Princeton University Press.

Tsing, A. (2017) "A Threat to Holocene Resurgence Is a Threat to Livability," in Brightman, M. and Lewis, J. (eds) *The Anthropology of Sustainability*. New York: Palgrave Macmillan, pp. 51–65. https://doi.org/10.1057/978.

Tsing, A. L., Bubandt, N., Gan, E., Swanson, H. A. (eds) (2017) *Arts of Living on a Damaged Planet: Arts of Living on a Damaged Planet Ghosts and Monsters of the Anthropocene*. Minneapolis: University of Minnesota Press. http://search.ebscohost.com/login.aspx?direct=true&scope=site&db=nlebk&db=nlabk&AN=1424665.

UN system task team on the post-2015 UN development dgenda (2012) *Realizing the Future We Want for All*.

UNESCO (1972) *Convention Concerning the Protection of the World Cultural and Natural Heritage*. Paris: UNESCO. [online], https://whc.unesco.org/en/conventiontext/ (accessed September 24, 2024).

UNESCO (2002) *Budapest Declaration on World Heritage*. Paris: UNESCO.

UNESCO (2003) *Convention for the Safeguarding of the Intangible Cultural Heritage*. Paris: UNESCO. [online], https://whc.unesco.org/en/documents/1334 (accessed September 24, 2024).

UNESCO (2005) *Convention on the Protection and Promotion of the Diversity of Cultural Expressions*. Paris: UNESCO. [online], https://www.unesco.org/

en/legal-affairs/convention-protection-and-promotion-diversity-cultural-expressions (accessed September 24, 2024).

UNESCO (2013) *Evaluation of UNESCO' s Standard-setting Work of the Culture Sector Part I – 2003 Convention for the Safeguarding of the Intangible Cultural Heritage October 2013.*

UNESCO (2020) "Operational Directives for the implementation of the Convention for the Safeguarding of the Intangible Heritage – Intangible Heritage – Culture Sector – UNESCO."

United Nations (1992) *Rio Declaration on Environment and Development.*

United Nations (2015) *Transforming Our World: The 2030 Agenda for Sustainable Development.* https://wedocs.unep.org/20.500.11822/9814.

Vidal, F. and Dias, N. (eds) (2016) *Endangerment, Biodiversity and Culture, Endangerment, Biodiversity and Culture.* London and New York: Routledge. https://doi.org/10.4324/9781315726823.

Villa, R. (2020) *Geel, la città dei matti. L'affidamento familiare dei malati mentali: sette secoli di storia.* Roma: Carocci.

Vlassis, A. (2015) "Culture in the Post-2015 Development Agenda: The Anatomy of an International Mobilisation," *Third World Quarterly*, 36(9), pp. 1649–1662. https://doi.org/10.1080/01436597.2015.1052064.

Voisenat, C. (2016) "Le tournant patrimonial," in Hottin, C. and Voisenat, C. (eds) *Le tournant patrimonial Mutations contemporaines des métiers du patrimoine.* Paris: Éditions de la Maison des sciences de l'homme, pp. 17–41.

Vuilleumier, J. and Hertz, E. (2024) "No Sustainability without Materiality: Complex Paths to Good Practices in Switzerland," in Bortolotto, C. and Skounti, A. (eds) *Intangible Cultural heritage and Sustainable Development: Inside a UNESCO Convention.* London: Routledge, pp. 127–142.

Wiktor-Mach, D. (2019) "Cultural Heritage and Development: UNESCO's New Paradigm in a Changing Geopolitical Context," *Third World Quarterly*, 40(9), pp. 1593–1612. https://doi.org/10.1080/01436597.2019.1604131.

Wiktor-Mach, D. (2020) "What Role for Culture in the Age of Sustainable Development? UNESCO's Advocacy in the 2030 Agenda Negotiations," *International Journal of Cultural Policy*, 26(3), pp. 312–327. https://doi.org/10.1080/10286632.2018.1534841.

Winter, T. (2013) "Clarifying the Critical in Critical Heritage Studies," *International Journal of Heritage Studies*, 19(6), pp. 532–545. https://doi.org/10.1080/13527258.2012.720997.

World Commission on Culture and Development (1996) *Our Creative Diversity: Report of the World Commission on Culture and Development.* Paris: UNESCO.

World Commission on Environment and Development (1987) *Report of the World Commission on Environment and Development: Our common future.* Oxford: Oxford University Press. https://sustainabledevelopment.un.org/milestones/wced.

Acknowledgments

As with any anthropological endeavor, my research heavily depends on the collaboration of my interlocutors in the field. I am therefore deeply indebted to current and former staff of the UNESCO secretariat for our enlightening discussions on ICH and SD over the last ten years. I would like to thank in particular (in alphabetical order) Irina Bokova, Tim Curtis, Helena Drobna, Cécile Duvelle, Susanne Schnüttgen, Hugues Sicard, and Rieks Smeets. It would be impossible to list the numerous experts and delegates from the 183 States Parties of the Convention with whom I have spoken about ICH and its governance throughout my research. I limit myself to mentioning here those that are quoted in this volume: Marc Jacobs, Jorijn Neyrinck, and Julien Vuillemier. Each of them encouraged inspiring intellectual debate, as well as provided access to unique opportunities for participant observation that enhanced my understanding of the ICH apparatus, while they simultaneously coped with the awkward position of being research subjects.

Fieldwork and interviews on the Geel foster care tradition and on the Swiss system for the management of avalanche risks were made possible thanks to collaboration on the part of the foster care team, the archivist of the Geel Public Psychiatric Care Centre of the Geel Gasthuismuseum, the Swiss ICH Cantonal experts, researchers in the Davos Institute of Snow and Avalanche Research, and representatives of the Swiss Alpine Club and the Swiss Mountain Guides Association.

Students in the course "Heritage for Sustainable development" taught within the "Innovation, Human Development and Sustainability" Masters program at the University of Geneva helped me to clarify my thoughts and were the first discussants of my research findings. A number of invited presentations provided precious opportunities to present and adjust my arguments with students and colleagues with different disciplinary approaches and trained in various academic traditions. For the invitations that enabled these stimulating interactions, I thank Nicolas Adell (Université de Toulouse – Jean Jaurès), Crisitina Amescua (Universidad Nacional Autónoma de México), Arnaud Chandivert (Université Paul-Valéry Montpellier), Christian Hottin (École Universitaire de Recherche Humanités, Création, Patrimoine, CY Cergy Paris Université), Kristin Kuutma (Universty of Tartu and University of St. Andrews), Manuel Peters (Brandenburgische Technische Universität Cottbus-Senftenberg), Céline Regnard (Aix-Marseille Université), Xavier Roigé (Universitat de Barcelona), Sylvie Sanges (Centre National de la Recherche Scientifique), Sophie Starrenburg (Tilburg Law School), and Ju Xi (Beijing National University).

Beyond the academic world, I benefited from the reactions of heritage professionals and representatives of civil society organizations in symposia and meetings. To this regard, I am grateful to the Académie Royale du Maroc, the Association Nationale des *Villes et Pays* d'*Art* et d'Histoire, the Archive of Ethnography and Social History of the Lombardy Region, the Centro de Pesquisa e Formação do Serviço Social do Comércio, the Forum of NGOs in Official Partnership with UNESCO, the ICH NGO Forum, the National Academy of Arts of Ukraine, and the Silk Road International Cultural Expo.

Janet Blake, Bernard Debarbieux, Séverine Cachat, Francesca Cozzolino, Harriet Deacon, Philip Demgenski, Florence Graezer Bideau, Lily Martinet, Hanna Schriber, and Ahmed Skounti offered insightful remarks on sections of this Element, and Christoph Brumann and Peter Larsen commented on the final manuscript. Maya Judd provided linguistic editing and Bhavani Vijayamani the project management. I am appreciative of their support and suggestions.

This work would have not been possible without generous funding from the CY Initiative of Excellence (grant "Investissements d'Avenir" ANR-16-IDEX-008) overseen by CY Advanced Studies. I also gratefully acknowledge the support of the French ministry of Culture, the Centre National de la Recherche Scientifique, and the research unit "Héritages: Culture/s, Patrimoine/s, Création/s." The research on Avalanche Risks Management was financed by the Collaborative Research on Science and Society (CROSS) Program, at the École Polytechnique Fédérale de Lausanne.

Cambridge Elements

Critical Heritage Studies

Kristian Kristiansen
University of Gothenburg

Michael Rowlands
UCL

About the Series

This series focuses on the recently established field of Critical Heritage Studies. Interdisciplinary in character, it brings together contributions from experts working in a range of fields, including cultural management, anthropology, archaeology, politics, and law. The series will include volumes that demonstrate the impact of contemporary theoretical discourses on heritage found throughout the world, raising awareness of the acute relevance of critically analysing and understanding the way heritage is used today to form new futures.

Cambridge Elements

Critical Heritage Studies

Elements in the Series

Native Americans in British Museums: Living Histories
Jack Davy

Understanding Islam at European Museums
Magnus Berg and Klas Grinell

Ethnographic Returns: Memory Processes and Archive Film
Anne Gustavsson

Global Heritage, Religion, and Secularism
Trinidad Rico

Heritage Making and Migrant Subjects in the Deindustrialising Region of the Latrobe Valley
Alexandra Dellios

Heritage and Design: Ten Portraits from Goa (India)
Pamila Gupta

Heritage, Education and Social Justice
Veysel Apaydin

Geopolitics of Digital Heritage
Natalia Grincheva and Elizabeth Stainforth

Here and Now at Historic Sites: Pupils and Guides Experiencing Heritage
David Ludvigsson, Martin Stolare and Cecilia Trenter

Heritage and Transformation of an African Popular Music
Aghi Bahi

The Neoliberalisation of Heritage in Africa
Rachel King

Will Heritage Save Us?: Intangible Cultural Heritage and the Sustainable Development Turn
Chiara Bortolotto

A full series listing is available at: www.cambridge.org/CHSE

www.ingramcontent.com/pod-product-compliance
Ingram Content Group UK Ltd.
Pitfield, Milton Keynes, MK11 3LW, UK
UKHW022145080726
473066UK00010B/760

* 9 7 8 1 0 0 9 5 0 9 1 0 7 *